THE MODERN ENNEAGRAM

The Modern
ENNEAGRAM

DISCOVER WHO YOU ARE
& WHO YOU CAN BE

Kacie Berghoef and Melanie Bell

ALTHEA
PRESS

CONTENTS

Introduction **7**

1 DISCOVERING
  THE SELF **10**

2 THE ENNEAGRAM
  IN PRACTICE **58**

3 THE ENNEAGRAM
  AT WORK **78**

4 THE ENNEAGRAM
  IN RELATIONSHIPS **108**

5 GROWTH AND
  CHANGE **134**

Conclusion **155**

Appendix: Shortcuts for Breaking Out of Your Box **157**

Resources **161**

References **164**

Index **167**

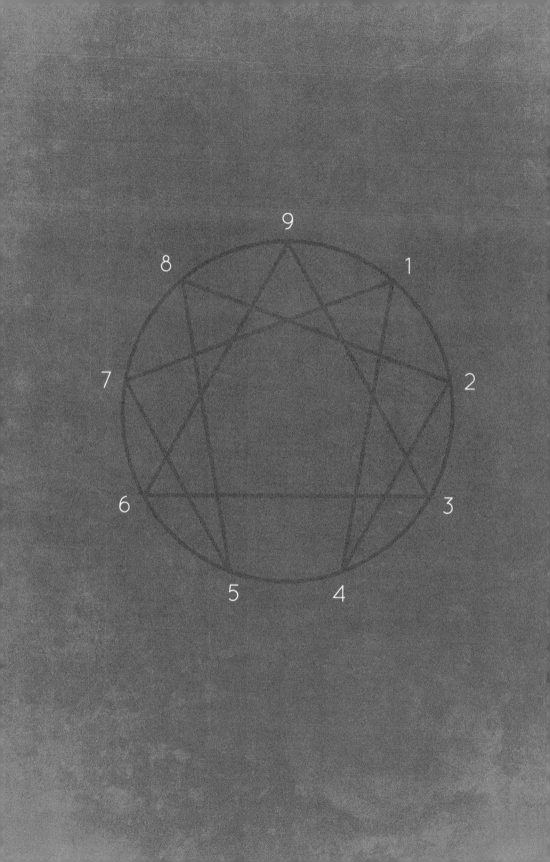

INTRODUCTION

Have you ever had an experience of realization—where you understood something about yourself and the world on a deeper level than you ever had before? Maybe this insight came from a moment of contemplation, or from new information that led you to look at things with fresh eyes. We'd like to introduce you to a personality system that has had this profound effect on us: the Enneagram.

Melanie's Story

When I first learned about the Enneagram, I was sitting with my friends at a long table in a college cafeteria, eating forkfuls of fried tofu and undercooked rice. I was a newly independent undergraduate student, fascinated by a personality workshop I'd just experienced in class and the discussion that had ensued—a discussion about how each participant saw the world differently. I wondered if personality psychology held the key I'd been seeking to understanding myself, making congruent choices, and connecting with others.

"Have you heard of the Enneagram?" one of my friends asked. He proceeded to give one-sentence descriptions of each type, and when I was unsure of mine, he handed me an Enneagram book to borrow. The system seemed complicated, and its geometric layout a little intimidating, until I started reading about the types. Not this one, not this one. . . Oh. Wait a minute. Had the authors been following me around with a video camera?

Ten years of Enneagram study and teaching later, this apt personality system maintains its power to surprise.

Kacie's Story

My story of self-discovery started on the Internet. My fascination with learning about how others worked began at a young age. By reading about various systems of personality and taking tests to determine my own type, I started to piece together why I, and others around me, acted in the way they did.

But everything deepened when a friend suggested I look into the Enneagram. A quick Internet search took me to The Enneagram Institute's website—and a powerful understanding. Coming face to face with the Enneagram descriptions, a whole new world opened up into the whys of my actions. It seemed like the Enneagram knew me better than I knew myself! As I dove into exploring the Enneagram and finding myself, the other personality systems I'd learned from, such as the Myers-Briggs Type Indicator and DiSC (an assessment that focuses on the traits of dominance, inducement, submission, and compliance), almost instantaneously dissolved into the background.

Fast forward over a decade, and I find that no matter how much inner work I've done and how much I think I know, I continue to be astonished and awed by the Enneagram's power and ability to know me.

A Tool for Growth

So what exactly does the Enneagram do? In short, it offers insight into nine distinct personality types. In a way, it's a window into why people do what we do.

The Enneagram explains how different people see the world, allowing us to understand where other people are coming from. From that standpoint, it's helpful for communication, workplace interaction, and relationship building. It's also a deeply growth-oriented concept, in that it describes habits of thought and behavior for each personality type—habits that keep many people stuck under day-to-day stresses— and offers ways to break out of those boxes. These growth paths are, in our opinion, one of the most important ways people can apply the system to themselves.

The Enneagram has been used to build understanding between family members and coworkers, forge bonds between South African leaders of different racial backgrounds post-apartheid, reduce recidivism rates for parolees, and open paths of communication between Israelis and Palestinians. For the two of us, it's helped with emotion management, self-acceptance, career development, relationship dynamics, and understanding our families. When used to promote understanding rather than stereotypes, the Enneagram is an immensely powerful tool.

A lot of our Enneagram learning came from books that remain fantastic and relevant, but haven't quite kept up with our fast-paced modern life. The world is changing quickly, and there are new ways to apply the Enneagram in our increasingly globalized, digitally connected world. The Enneagram is used in more business and personal contexts with every passing year.

In this book, you'll learn the basics of the history and theory of the Enneagram, as well as how its intricate parts work together. Then, you'll discover how to apply these insights to your work, relationships, and daily life. We'll give you a very practical overview of what the Enneagram is and what it does. We'll point you to resources where you can learn more, including personality tests that will help you discover your type. We encourage you to read about all nine personality types with an open mind, and pay attention to which one resonates with you the most.

Are you ready to join us on an Enneagram journey? Let's get started!

DISCOVERING THE SELF

The Enneagram is more than a flash-in-the-pan personality test. With historical roots dating back to at least the fourteenth century, the modern Enneagram has helped thousands of people discover truths about themselves and their life's purpose. Not only is it an interesting way to learn about yourself, but it's also a catalyst for inspiration and transformation.

The insights that the Enneagram offers can help with many practical life decisions, such as finding a career or lifestyle that suits your personality best. As you learn about your type and watch how it shows up in your life, you may discover that you thrive in a calmer environment than you're currently living in or that your talents would be best used in more people-oriented work than you're doing now. You might recognize habits that get in the way of being your best self, and, as a result, make changes over time.

You'll also find the Enneagram useful as a guide for understanding others. Knowing the personality types of the people around you can help you better understand your family, resolve conflict with your partner, and communicate more effectively with your coworkers. The Enneagram offers such a vast amount of wisdom that these days, many therapists, coaches, business consultants, and spiritual teachers choose to use this system to support the people they serve.

In this chapter, we'll talk a little bit about the history of the Enneagram and how it developed from an ancient symbol into the practical psychospiritual tool we use today. We'll look at the various parts of the Enneagram symbol and their significance. Then, we'll give an overview of the nine Enneagram types, as well as the core motivations, gifts, and challenges each type possesses. Read on for a deep dive into the human psyche, and a first glimpse at how to harness this powerful knowledge for your own personal growth.

Spiritual Roots: The Enneagram in History

The nine-pointed Enneagram symbol is said to originate from Sufism, a mystical branch of Islam, and was first popularized in the West by Russian spiritual teacher G. I. Gurdjieff in the early twentieth century. He taught the Enneagram as a way of understanding the movements and changes that constitute the spiritual dimension of life. The Enneagram also formed the foundation of some of the sacred dances he guided his students to perform. Gurdjieff's dances, based on precise and intentional movements, aimed to cultivate attention and awareness. A key aspect of Gurdjieff's teaching was identifying his students' "chief feature," a prominent psychodynamic behavior pattern that kept them "asleep" to their true nature. He used this knowledge to personalize his teaching to each student, guiding them on individual paths toward spiritual growth that balanced their mental, physical, and emotional faculties.

Bolivian transpersonal teacher Oscar Ichazo incorporated the idea of people having a weakness or flaw in their point of view into the Enneagram itself. In the 1950s, he developed a system of mapping personality types around the Enneagram, creating the foundation for today's widespread Enneagram teachings. His system was predicated on opposites: For each of the nine personality types, he assigned a corresponding passion (or emotional imbalance) and virtue.

PSYCHOLOGICAL INSIGHTS

In the 1970s, psychiatrist Claudio Naranjo developed Ichazo's ideas further, sketching profiles of each type's psychodynamics and describing common type-related pathologies. For each type, he identified motivations, cognitive biases, and neurotic tendencies, such as narcissism or histrionic traits. He was also the first person to use the panel method of teaching. He grouped individuals by type and asked them questions, enabling both Naranjo and his students to get a better understanding of each Type. For example, he would assemble a group of individuals who identified with Type One and ask them questions, illuminating aspects of the type for his audience. This approach to the Enneagram is widely used today.

Naranjo taught his Enneagram material to students in Berkeley, California, as he developed it. His insights spread to Jesuit seminaries where they were further disseminated. The first generation of Enneagram authors learned the Enneagram mostly from this transmission. Maria Beesing, Robert Nogosek, and Patrick O'Leary published the first book on the Enneagram as a personality system, called *The Enneagram*, in 1984. You may be familiar with the others that followed, such as Don Riso's *Personality Types* and Helen Palmer's *The Enneagram: Understanding Yourself and Others in Your Life*.

THE ENNEAGRAM TODAY

Both Riso and Palmer became leaders in the field and founders of the world's most prominent Enneagram school. Don Riso expanded descriptions of the psychology of each type to include nine Levels of Development, differentiating healthy, average, and unhealthy manifestations of the types. These span the whole range of human potential, from optimal functioning to psychological pathology. Riso founded The Enneagram Institute and partnered with Russ Hudson to further develop his work. Riso's contemporary Helen Palmer wrote additional books about practical Enneagram applications and founded the Narrative Tradition. In this influential school, Palmer and her teaching partner David Daniels refined Naranjo's panel approach—where groups of a certain type were brought together—using personal stories to provide both an understanding of type and a healing experience for panelists.

Knowledge of the Enneagram as a personality system has spread beyond its esoteric roots and entered the mainstream. Across the globe, therapists, coaches, and corporate trainers use the Enneagram with their clients. While we are certified and authorized teachers with The Enneagram Institute and our understanding is deeply influenced by this school's psychodynamic approach, we have studied with Enneagram professionals who apply the system to fields as diverse as executive coaching and hypnosis. Over the next few chapters, we'll give you a sense of the diverse ways the Enneagram can be applied.

The Structure of the Enneagram

Though represented as a simple figure, the Enneagram's numbers, circles, and lines can be interpreted many different ways. Let's take a look at the Enneagram form most people know:

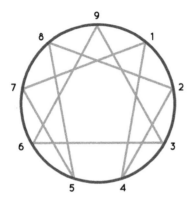

CIRCLE The nine points of the Enneagram figure (each representing one of the nine types) are enclosed within a circle. The circle represents unity, showing that all nine Enneagram types are equal and connected to one another.

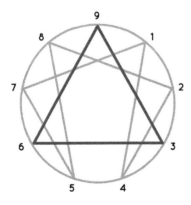

TRIANGLE The Enneagram's inner triangle, which connects three points, represents a dynamic interaction of three forces. Think of any pair of opposites; the third point, or force, represents a synthesis or middle ground that brings them together. Three Enneagram types—Types Three, Six, and Nine—are connected by the triangle.

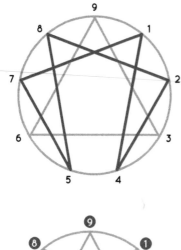

HEXAD The hexad is an irregular figure that connects the other six points. Its structure represents dynamism and change. While we all have a dominant personality type, we are also in constant flux. Six Enneagram types—Types One, Two, Four, Five, Seven, and Eight—are connected by the hexad.

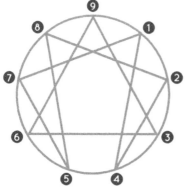

NUMBERS The nine numbers around the circle represent the nine Enneagram personality types. Each Enneagram type has a different core motivation that drives behavior. Every person has aspects of all the types within them, but everyone also has a *primary* Enneagram type—a type that impacts an individual's perceptions, actions, and interpretations of the world.

THE ENNEAGRAM'S ARROWS

Many types on the Enneagram are interconnected, sometimes with arrows. These arrows follow a precise structure that reflects the shifts people go through under stress, in secure situations, and as they follow a path of personal growth. When we move to one of our connecting points, we take on some of that type's behaviors. This movement is seamless and can happen multiple times in any given day.

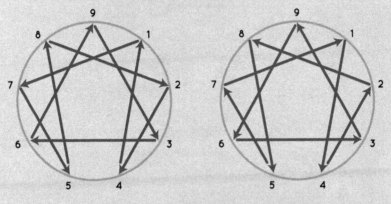

SECURITY POINTS   STRESS POINTS

The backward-pointing arrows show each type's **Stress Point**, the type we move to when we feel under stress. Moving to our Stress Point can give us a break from our usual way of acting and prevent us from becoming less healthy. Under severe stress, some people can move to their Stress Point and stay there for months or years.

The forward-pointing arrows show each type's **Security Point**, which allows us to act out the behaviors of another type for a while. Security Point movement usually happens in situations that feel familiar and trustworthy or when we are healthy, a movement known as our **Integration Point**. We integrate qualities of that type that help balance our own, such as confidence or structure. To change and grow, we need to develop our Security Point's healthy behaviors in our daily lives.

THE CENTERS AND TRIADS

The Enneagram types can be organized into several different triads, or groupings of three. These triads describe commonalities between types, such as their dominant intelligence, social style, conflict resolution style, and object relations. A summary of each group of triads and how each triad works is given next.

THE THREE CENTERS

The nine Enneagram types are represented by three different centers of intelligence: the Gut Center, Heart Center, and Head Center. When we are balanced, we have equal use and access to all three intelligence centers, allowing us to access powerful strengths. All of us possess these three centers, but one of them is dominant in shaping our personality type's strengths and challenges. While the dominant center holds powerful abilities, it also has the most potential to be overused or misused.

THE GUT CENTER focuses on our physical instincts and bodies. Noticing our bodily sensations brings us incredible somatic intelligence. When we listen to our physical instincts, we feel strong, physically embodied, and anchored in the present moment. When our Gut Center is underused, we feel ungrounded and have a difficult time asserting ourselves. Types One, Eight, and Nine comprise the Gut Triad. These types, at their best, are independent with strong physical boundaries. When out of balance, they feel they must assert their will over others, and they struggle with anger.

THE HEART CENTER focuses on our personal identity and values. Listening to our hearts gives us strong emotional intelligence. When we open up and listen to our hearts, we become compassionate, feel our own personal sense of self, and release our past hurts. When our Heart Center is underused, we feel cut off from our feelings and have trouble seeing who we truly are. Types Two, Three, and Four comprise the Heart Triad. These types, at their best, are compassionate and have a strong sense of self. When out of balance, they feel they must develop an identity through outside validation, and they struggle with shame.

THE HEAD CENTER focuses on obtaining knowing and support. Quieting our minds brings us powerful internal guidance. When we clear our heads, we gain contact with our inner knowing, learning the best way for us to move forward into the future. When our Head Center is underused, our minds are foggy, and we follow external guidance instead of our inner guide. Types Five, Six, and Seven comprise the Head Triad. These types, at their best, are clear-minded and in touch with their powerful inner guidance. When out of balance, they believe they must seek security through other means, and they struggle with anxiety.

THE SOCIAL STYLES

Named by Don Riso and Russ Hudson, the Hornevian Triads describe three distinct social styles the Enneagram types tend to use as they move through life. It uses psychologist Karen Horney's three trends of moving against, moving toward, and moving away to describe assertive, compliant, and withdrawn personalities on the Enneagram.

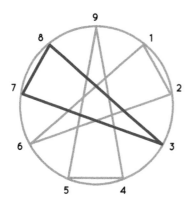

THE ASSERTIVE TRIAD. Types Three, Seven, and Eight fit Horney's classic social style of moving against others. Types that use this style tend to be doers and bring the strength of getting things moving. They focus on taking action and resolving situations quickly. Interpersonally, their assertiveness gives them the easiest time of the styles confronting and speaking their minds with other people. Sometimes, people of these types, in particular, can come off as overly brusque, with the potential to hurt others' feelings.

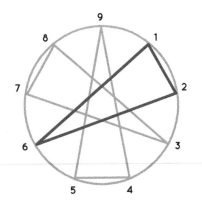

THE COMPLIANT TRIAD. Types One, Two, and Six fit Horney's classic social style of moving toward others. Types that use this style tend to be dutiful and bring the strength of strong cooperation with others. They focus on providing support and assistance. Interpersonally, these types tend to convey warmth and a desire to please, and they can "lean in" in order to read your needs. Sometimes these types can come off as overly focused on social rules in interactions, with the potential of irritating others.

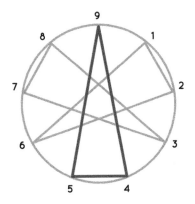

THE WITHDRAWN TRIAD. Types Four, Five, and Nine fit Horney's classic social style of moving away from others. Types that use this style tend to have a focus that is at once internal, and also broad, strategic, and global. Interpersonally, these types tend to be thoughtful, self-contained, and are often (although not always) more introverted than the other two styles. Sometimes, these types have a difficult time speaking up and expressing themselves in social situations, leaving others confused as to their needs and desires.

THE CONFLICT RESOLUTION STYLES

All of us encounter conflict, challenges, and decisions in our lives. We react to these events unconsciously and according to our Enneagram type. There are three basic styles we use to manage day-to-day conflicts. These styles—Competency, Emotional Realness, and Positive Outlook—form what Riso and Hudson call the Harmonic Triads. Three Enneagram types each prefer one of the harmonic styles, and all of the styles have valuable strengths and challenges associated with them.

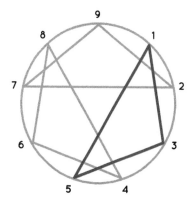

THE COMPETENCY TRIAD. Competency Types—One, Three, and Five—are natural problem solvers. When faced with a conflict or challenge, they aim to stay civil and immediately strategize to find solutions. These types are excellent at long-term planning and keeping themselves or a group on track to reaching a goal. The downside is that these types can be overly focused and emotionally restricted. When we solve conflicts analytically, we avoid either feeling immediate emotions or viewing the situation positively. This means these types don't always take emotional needs and the broader context of the problem into account when decisions are made, making some solutions less useful than they could be.

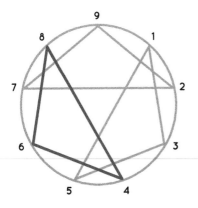

THE EMOTIONAL REALNESS TRIAD.
Emotional Realness Types—Four, Six, and Eight—are skilled at drawing out emotions and feelings. In conflicts and challenges, they first want to process their feelings and hear emotional responses from others, in order to bring pressing needs to the surface. This allows difficult feelings, conflicts, and challenges out into the open, clearing the air to move forward. The downside is that these types can have difficulty moving forward; addressing feelings is productive initially, but has the potential to spiral into endless conflict and emotional processing, making it hard to see the positivity in the situation or implement solutions.

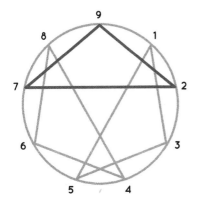

THE POSITIVE OUTLOOK TRIAD.
Positive Outlook Types—Two, Seven, and Nine—excel at making the best out of any challenge and having a broad view—a view where the problem is not such a big deal. Seeing positivity and finding hope in even dark times helps us keep our spirits up and keep going under duress. The downside to this style is that it can lead to denial that a conflict or challenge is even taking place. Denial makes it hard to air out feelings or develop solutions to the challenge. Not addressing a conflict can cause it to grow bigger than it would have if it had been acknowledged right away.

THE OBJECT RELATIONS TRIADS

All of us have certain ways of relating to other people. These tend to be unconscious and deeply ingrained in us from a young age. First described in psychodynamic theory, object relations patterns can be categorized into three groups: attachment, rejection, and frustration. Each of these is a dominant pattern of relating to others for three Enneagram types. When we overidentify with these patterns, it's difficult for us to act consciously in our relationships. By understanding these patterns in ourselves, we can start to identify when our reactions to others come from our own deeply held psychological defense strategies rather than from the interaction itself.

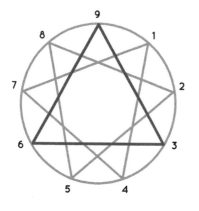

THE ATTACHMENT TRIAD reflects how we all attach and attempt to remain in a flow with the world around us. Types Three, Six, and Nine tend to focus on attaching to and then maintaining a certain internal state. This ranges from attachment to others' desires, to attachment to external support, to attachment to a sense of inner peace. These types' defense mechanisms strive to keep things just the way they are.

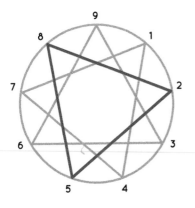

THE REJECTION TRIAD reflects the strategies we use for survival in the world. Types Two, Five, and Eight feel rejected by the world and like they need to bring something to others. Their strategies include offering people their love and service, their knowledge and expertise, and their strong protection. These types' defense mechanisms attempt to gain acceptance while assuming the individual will not receive it.

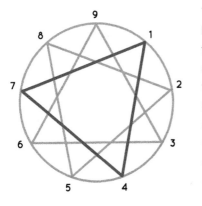

THE FRUSTRATION TRIAD describes how all of us try to get what we want from the world. Types One, Four, and Seven tend to feel chronically frustrated—like they are never able to get their needs met. This frustration may stem from the world's lack of morality, other people's deviation from an idealized view of them, or a low supply of excitement. These types' defenses seek an ideal rather than savoring lived experience.

TEST TAKING AND
FINDING YOUR TYPE

This book doesn't offer a self-test, but taking a type assessment is a shortcut that can point you toward a likely Enneagram type. If you don't know your type, there is a variety of resources you can check out before digging into this book. Here are a few:

ENNEAGRAM TYPING TESTS

▸ The Enneagram Institute's RHETI (Riso-Hudson Enneagram Type Indicator) is a scientifically validated Enneagram assessment, available for $10 at enneagraminstitute.com. We recommend it if you're interested in a thorough test, but you'll have to read about your type on the website or elsewhere since the assessment doesn't include a detailed report.

▸ Enneagram in the Narrative Tradition offers a scientifically validated, paragraph-based Enneagram assessment initially developed by David Daniels, MD, and Virginia Price, PhD. It includes educational videos about your top type results as a tool to guide your selection. It's available at enneagramworldwide.com for $10.

▸ Jerry Wagner, PhD, developed the WEPSS (Wagner Enneagram Personality Style Scales), a scientifically standardized, reliable, and validated assessment. In addition to covering your primary type, it explains your connections to other types through the Enneagram's arrows and wings. It's available for $10 at WEPSS.com.

▸ Integrative Enneagram Solutions offers an Enneagram test using Integrative Intelligent Questionnaire Technology. The test and a brief type report are $15 at integrative.co.za. The company also offers Enneagram-based assessment of teams and their level of functioning.

- Ginger Lapid-Bogda, PhD, developed an app with an animated Enneagram test called Know Your Type. The app also features videos, personal development activities, and tips for interacting with other types. Download it for $3.99 at enneagramapp.com.

OTHER WAYS TO DISCOVER YOUR TYPE

- **Get feedback from family and friends.** Sometimes our loved ones see our patterns more clearly than we do. Don't be afraid to ask trusted confidantes what strengths, gifts, and traits you bring to the world.

- **Consult an expert.** Many certified Enneagram teachers offer typing interviews that assist you in discovering your type. Since these consultations are tailored to you, this is often a quick way to find your type.

- **Read the descriptions in this book.** If one of the type descriptions stands out and resonates with you, it just might be your type!

- **Test results vs. self-knowledge.** In some cases, an Enneagram test will indicate one type for you, but you may identify more strongly with a different type after reading the descriptions. No Enneagram test is completely accurate, and self-recognition is the best way to find your type. We recommend reading up on your top three test results, as there are many reasons you might test as one type while being another: cultural or family expectations, gender roles, a more positive view of certain traits, and so on. Look for the type that resonates with you at your best *and* worst. It's also useful to get feedback from friends and family members, who may know you better than you know yourself!

THE WINGS

The Enneagram may only have nine basic types, but each type has a number of variations. The wings are one factor that brings diversity to how we each express our dominant Enneagram type. Your wing is one of two types next to your dominant Enneagram type. For example, if you are a Three, your two possible wings are Type Two and Type Four. Most people only have one dominant wing, although some Enneagram teachers believe there are people who use both wings equally.

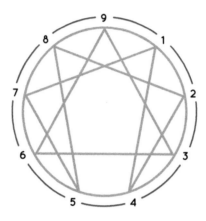

Your wing does not change our dominant Enneagram type's core motivations or traits. However, it does modify the way your type appears, adding a certain "flavor" of a secondary personality type. Two people with the same type and different wings can look quite distinct. A Four with a Three Wing, for example, may appear dramatic and flamboyant next to a more reserved and intellectually oriented Four with a Five Wing.

The wings are stronger and more visible in some people than others. A Six, for example, with a particularly strong Five or Seven Wing will appear closer to Type Five or Seven in behavior and personality traits, although they will still be a dominant Type Six. On the other hand, some Sixes will have a much weaker wing, to the point that the wing is difficult to see or discern.

Once you discover your wing, you can write your full type in shorthand as *(dominant type)w(wing type)*. For example, a Six with a

Five Wing is a 6w5, and a Six with a Seven Wing is a 6w7. Wings add diversity and precision to Enneagram types and help explain some of the variety we see within each type. As we introduce each personality type, we'll also highlight and differentiate between its wings.

The Nine Types

The nine Enneagram types are motivated by different core desires and use different strategies to meet these desires. They also have distinct gifts and challenges. While most Enneagram experts agree that people remain as one type through their lives, it is possible for anyone to manifest healthy, average, and unhealthy versions of their dominant type at different points in their lives—or even at different points of the day.

The following descriptions give an overview of what drives each personality type as well as various ways the types may act. They also differentiate between the most adaptive, balanced, and mindful (healthy) manifestations of the type; the day-to-day, functional "autopilot" (average) manifestations of the type; and the unbalanced, struggling (unhealthy) manifestations of each type. No Enneagram type exists in a void, so the profiles also illuminate each type's connections to other types through wings and arrows.

Why Nine? *The use of nine in the modern Enneagram personality system is rooted in a convergence of spiritual traditions. The idea of nine manifestations of divinity, reflected in nine "flavors" of humanity, dates back to The Enneads by the philosopher Plotinus. It's also reflected in the Kabbalistic Tree of Life, which has 10 sephiroth, or spheres, that souls originate from: Nine types of people, plus one sphere reserved for the Messiah. Ichazo synthesized the spheres of the Tree of Life with the Seven Deadly Sins, plus two additional sins (original to the source material), to map nine personality types around the Enneagram.*

TYPE ONE: SEEKING INTEGRITY

Ones on the Enneagram are motivated by strong principles and a desire for goodness. They envision a world that is ethical, just, and improved—a world that could be. No two Ones have the same vision. Some rally allies to reduce pollution and clean up habitats. Others maintain a vision of how to keep an ideal home, down to the details of proper towel folding and the organization of their spice racks. You can, and will, find Ones at all points on the political spectrum. What brings them together is their integrity and conscientiousness.

HEALTHY

Balanced Ones set a principled example for all of us. They "walk the talk" and live their values with grounded, embodied commitment. Their ability to instruct and speak to people's higher aspirations can motivate many to follow their ideals. In addition to being effective crusaders for change, their fairness and wisdom make them wonderful judges and impactful teachers. They are idealistic and continually touched by humanity's efforts toward improvement and truth.

AVERAGE

While balanced Ones bring acceptance and flexibility into their work and lives, average Ones feel a constant sense of personal responsibility. High-minded and idealistic, they feel dissatisfied with how things are in the present. This causes them to strive harder toward causes and ways of living that embody their personal ideals—not just a better future, but a perfect future. Their posture and mindset often become rigid and tense. Ones can become critical of small errors by anyone, including themselves. When stressed, their excessive moralizing and criticisms of others who do the "wrong" thing causes others to be resentful of them.

TYPE 1
SEEKING INTEGRITY

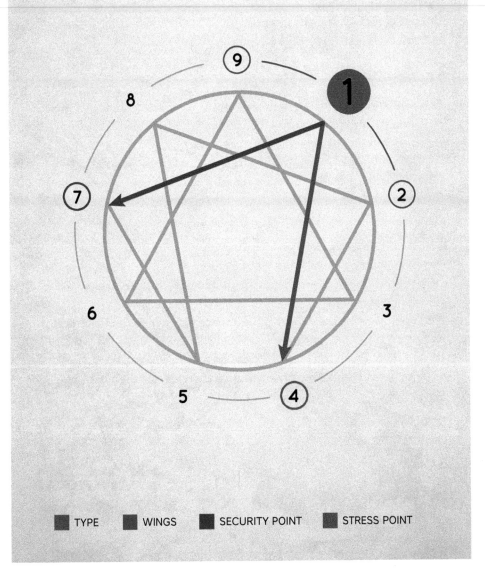

■ TYPE　　■ WINGS　　■ SECURITY POINT　　■ STRESS POINT

UNHEALTHY

When especially out of balance, Ones will go to extremes to enforce their version of "The Truth" on others. At this point, they may justify their own errors and secretly do the opposite of what they prescribe. This behavior can lead to severe obsessive-compulsive tendencies and nervous breakdowns.

It's helpful for Ones to adopt a more relaxed, patient outlook. Taking time to themselves and letting go of the little things will lessen the sense of pressure and self-criticism, allowing them to bring their mission more effectively into fruition.

WINGS

One with a Nine Wing (1w9): More aloof and intellectual, these Ones are often motivated by philosophical ideals. When balanced, they command an impartial sense of justice.

One with a Two Wing (1w2): More active and interpersonal, these Ones' principles tend to be more directly involved with people. The desire to help reinforces their desire for change.

ARROWS

Type One's Stress Point is the self-indulgent Type Four. Tired of being responsible, stressed-out Ones succumb to depressive feelings or indulge their cravings.

Type One's Security Point is the spontaneous Type Seven. In safe situations, Ones let their carefree, rebellious side fly free. Growth toward their Seven Integration Point allows Ones to get in touch with joy, humor, and a sense of lightness that relieves their conscientious striving.

TYPE TWO: SEEKING CONNECTION

Twos on the Enneagram are motivated by a desire to connect with others through loving, mutually nurturing relationships. They care deeply about other people and are adept at recognizing and meeting their needs. They might, for instance, learn and ask about the families of all the service people they see in their daily life. They may extend a helping hand by cooking special meals, connecting members of their network who will benefit from knowing each other, giving personalized attention, or offering heartfelt support in various other ways.

HEALTHY

Balanced Twos are open and naturally empathetic. Deeply attuned to others, they are generous and know how to attune to people with kindness. They derive selfless joy from these connections. In work settings, they excel at mentoring and coaching. Their altruism extends to themselves as well; they value self-love and know when and how to nurture themselves. Many healthy Twos become teachers of self-care and are free to develop complementary, less interpersonal gifts, such as scholarship or artistry.

AVERAGE

Average Twos are warm and friendly toward others. Rather than giving openly and selflessly, they "lean in" to others and seek needs to fulfill. This can manifest through traditional caregiving or other forms of help. They derive a strong sense of value from pleasing and serving others and start to desire approval in return. Twos can become manipulative, creating and fulfilling needs for others and wanting others to be dependent on their help. Overbearing and self-important behavior can cause others to be exasperated by Twos' "help" and reject their advances.

TYPE 2
SEEKING
CONNECTION

TYPE   WINGS   SECURITY POINT   STRESS POINT

UNHEALTHY

When unhealthy, Twos seek love and appreciation at all costs and will aggressively coerce others into feeling guilty and taking their help. At this point, Twos can resort to extreme "give to get" behavior that can lead to stalking and victimizing others, or physically falling apart from self-neglect.

It's useful for Twos to make a habit of tuning in to their own feelings and physical impulses when they feel their energy flowing outward. Connecting with themselves allows for authentic connections to develop.

WINGS

Two with a One Wing (2w1): These Twos tend to be more dutiful and directly service-focused people. They feel their helping is serving a cause. Some take pride in simplicity.

Two with a Three Wing (2w3): These Twos are more image-oriented people, and their helping is often more outward. They use charm and flair to engage others.

ARROWS

Type Two's Stress Point is the aggressive Type Eight. When exhausted from tending to other people's needs, Twos become bossy and overbearing toward others.

Type Two's Security Point is the self-aware Type Four. In safe situations, Twos feel comfortable expressing their more difficult emotions. Growth toward their Four Integration Point allows Twos to connect deeply with who they are and balance their love of others with self-healing.

TYPE THREE: SEEKING VALUE

Enneagram Threes are driven by a need to shine, to exemplify and embody a personal sense of value. We see Threes who are proficient in many disciplines. The Three umbrella includes efficient and accomplished businesspeople, athletes, celebrities, spiritual guides, rebels, and parents. In any area of life that can be done well, you likely know of a Three who excels. Self-assured and adaptable, Threes wow others with their achievements and grace. They are often inspirations for others to believe in themselves and follow their own dreams.

HEALTHY

Healthy Threes shine with authentic value. Their actions and behaviors reflect their truest inner selves. They have open hearts, and combine their talents with humility and service. They are aware of their adaptability and ease with flexible self-presentation. Some Threes use this gift playfully, engaging performance techniques to open people's eyes to a world of glittering possibilities. Some employ it persuasively as spokespeople or advocates. Hardworking and driven toward their dreams, balanced Threes bring out the best in themselves and others.

AVERAGE

Average Threes are goal-oriented and often accomplished, but they define their success in terms of external measures rather than their own hearts. They are attuned to the desires of others around them and will easily adapt themselves to other's expectations in order to succeed. Highly focused on outcomes, they will do what's needed to get things done. Even so, their facade can start to seem overly glossy. They may come off as phony and overly status-oriented to others, while losing touch with their own authentic personal desires in the name of external success. They can become narcissistic, arrogant show-offs with grandiose views of themselves.

TYPE 3
SEEKING VALUE

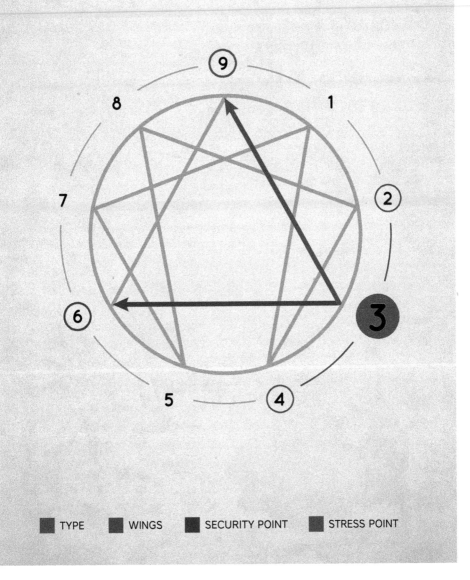

TYPE   WINGS   SECURITY POINT   STRESS POINT

UNHEALTHY

Unhealthy Threes seek success at all costs, going to extreme lengths to avoid public failure, including behind-the-scenes behaviors that are "dirty" and exploitive of others. At this point, they can become malicious and vengeful, destroying anyone in the way of their success and goals.

It's important for Threes to connect with their own feelings and desires, especially in ways that don't involve the public eye. Listening to their hearts will thaw Threes' coolness and unleash their deepest, most powerfully real potential.

WINGS

Three with a Two Wing (3w2): More outgoing and affable, Threes with a Two Wing enjoy motivating and inspiring others. They are skilled at being "the face" of things.

Three with a Four Wing (3w4): More reserved and polished, Threes with a Four Wing enjoy presenting themselves in a distinctive way. They often have a professional edge.

ARROWS

Type Three's Stress Point is the passive Type Nine. When burnt out from striving for success, Threes grow listless and numb themselves by disengaging.

Type Three's Security Point is the committed Type Six. In safe situations, Threes let their anxiety show and may wonder if they're good enough. Growth toward their Six Integration Point helps Threes recognize the value of working for a greater good and become true team players.

TYPE FOUR: SEEKING IDENTITY

Enneagram Fours are motivated by the desire to know themselves fully. They are seekers attuned to the realm of subjectivity. Willing to delve into the depths of their emotions, they possess resilience and creativity. Through art, teaching, emotional connection, and other forms of engagement in the world, Fours point others toward universal truths of internal life. Their self-awareness often results in meaningful and uniquely personal forms of expression. They recognize and share the beauty they find in the inner and outer worlds.

HEALTHY

All Fours have innate sensitivity. In healthy Fours, this sensitivity is accompanied by emotional fortitude. Balanced Fours are supportive companions in facing your darkest shadows; they know and accept the terrain. Whether a friend, therapist, manager, or other confidant, a Four is emotionally honest and apt to handle other people's feelings with gentleness and compassion. They live in a way that's true to themselves. Their ability to connect with their own hearts creates an easy flow of expression. With the help of grounded self-discipline, balanced Fours can create resonant works of art and express mysterious, hard-to-define truths.

AVERAGE

While the creativity of balanced Fours is grounded in reality, average Fours are oriented to aesthetics and the imaginative. They are sensitive to their inner emotional landscape and will cultivate certain feelings as a way of maintaining a self-image. They often fantasize—a form of escapism that allows them to long for and seek a rescuer. They can become withdrawn, emotionally precious, and hypersensitive to any perceived slight from others. They may begin to feel that others are "normal" and they are not, driving envy and resentment toward others, as well as self-isolation, self-indulgence, and impracticality.

TYPE 4
SEEKING IDENTITY

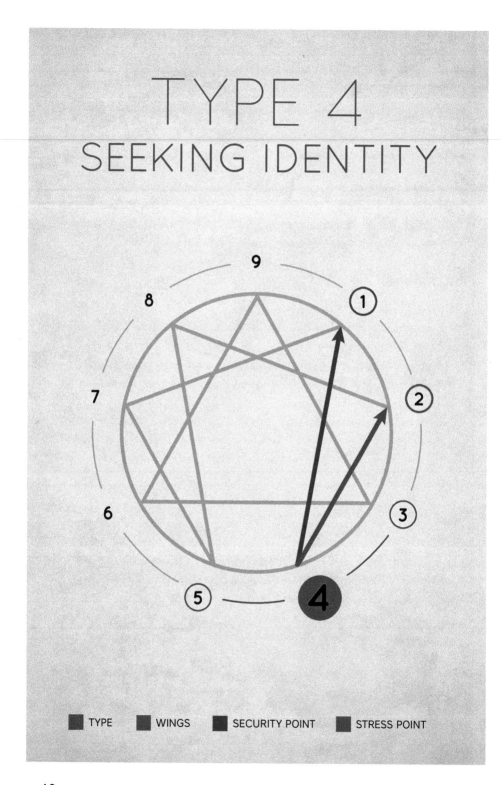

TYPE   WINGS   SECURITY POINT   STRESS POINT

UNHEALTHY

Unhealthy Fours become increasingly emotionally unstable while attempting to preserve their identity. They can grow frozen, self-hating, depressed, and unable to function. At this point, they can become self-abusive and hateful toward others, and are at risk for emotional breakdowns.

Fours benefit from creating structure in their lives. Using self-discipline, rather than following their feelings, will allow them to do what they truly want to do. Service and engagement with others will help them express their gifts in the world.

WINGS

Four with a Three Wing (4w3): These showier Fours are able to craft images and works that express their personal flair while connecting effectively with audiences.

Four with a Five Wing (4w5): These more intellectual Fours express their own ideas uncompromisingly, following an eclectic personal vision.

ARROWS

Type Four's Stress Point is the people-pleasing Type Two. When isolated and self-conscious, Fours move ingratiatingly toward others and try to meet their needs to regain connection.

Type Four's Security Point is the conscientious Type One. In safe situations, Fours feel comfortable expressing criticism of others. Growth toward their One Integration Point leads Fours to step into alignment with a sense of mission that extends beyond the self.

TYPE FIVE: SEEKING CLARITY

Fives on the Enneagram are in search of clarity and masterful knowledge. They are perceptive and able to bring together ideas, or generate new ones, in flashes of insight that appear surprisingly simple. Think of the simultaneous simplicity and inventiveness of recognizing gravity, or realizing that a minor key could make a tune convey a completely different effect. Fives are innovative and inventive, delighting in learning new things about areas of interest, committed to the meticulous reality testing and questioning process of discovery.

HEALTHY

Healthy Fives are highly original, with the potential to make discoveries that move humanity forward. They develop insightful theories and observations of the world. They are open-minded, and their deep understanding breeds compassion for others. They possess an objectivity that recognizes the transience of life and the importance of truth. Rather than getting attached to particular ideas, they look for what's real. While they are often specialists, researchers, and thinkers, the scope of their curiosity is wide. They learn from engagement and experience as much as they learn from study.

AVERAGE

Average Fives remain intellectually studious and mentally curious, but their scope is narrower. Highly focused, they become experts at whatever interests them. Their focus is learning, and they have trouble putting their ideas into action. Engaging in the external world becomes increasingly difficult, and they can grow detached, withdrawing into mental worlds and interests. Their isolation causes them to start to lose touch with reality. They may become mentally agitated and paranoid, developing extreme theories and views of reality that can provoke and disturb others.

TYPE 5
SEEKING CLARITY

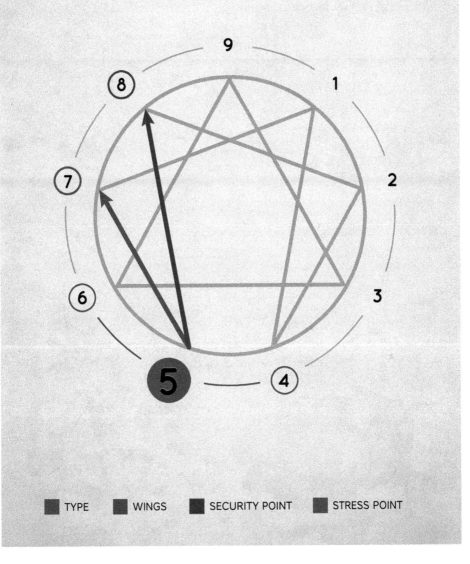

TYPE WINGS SECURITY POINT STRESS POINT

UNHEALTHY

Unhealthy Fives attempt to preserve their view of reality at any cost. They completely cut themselves off from others—and their own needs. At this point, their highly distorted thinking can cause delusions, depression, and self-destructive behavior, leaving them at risk for psychotic breaks.

Fives benefit from challenging themselves to take action before they've thought everything through. Fives never feel quite ready to act, but acting is often their richest path to discovery and clarity.

WINGS

Five with a Four Wing (5w4): These more inward-looking Fives bring subjective awareness to their process of analysis and discovery. They may enjoy the overtly bizarre.

Five with a Six Wing (5w6): These more outward-looking Fives bring rigorous, process-oriented thinking to their analytic methods. They may prefer systematizing or hands-on means.

ARROWS

Type Five's Stress Point is the scattered Type Seven. When tired out from being hyperfocused, Fives seek out sources of excitement and stimulation in the external world.

Type Five's Security Point is the confident Type Eight. In safe situations, Fives reveal their pushy, aggressive side. Growth toward their Eight Integration Point allows Fives to gain a stronger sense of groundedness and embodiment, taking action on their insights.

TYPE SIX: SEEKING GUIDANCE

Sixes on the Enneagram are motivated by a search for guidance. At their best, they connect with a clear sense of orientation and trust of themselves, which helps show others the way as well. Committed and stable, Sixes are dedicated allies and strong team-builders. They value collaboration and recognize that we are all interdependent. As leaders, they cultivate a spirit of teamwork. You can recognize the gifts of Type Sixes behind the trend of flat, nonhierarchical organizations, where members make decisions collectively and elevate each other.

HEALTHY

Healthy Sixes are exceedingly courageous people. They recognize when they are called toward a mission and bring tenacity and determination to see it through. Fully aware of their fear and apprehension, they do not let it stop them from taking vital action. Through this lesson, they teach others to trust their own internal GPS and to differentiate true guidance from less accurate sources of advice—rightfully regarded with skepticism. Balanced Sixes are engaging, warm, and likeable. They have a sense of humor and relatability that people love being around.

AVERAGE

While healthy Sixes trust that things will work out, average Sixes worry about what could go wrong. They are hard workers who create systems and troubleshoot in organizations. They begin looking for external sources of security and guidance. By committing to too many things, Sixes can become overworked and spread too thin. They start to test what they've committed to, to see if it can be trusted. Ambivalence, reactivity, and push-pull behaviors make others uncertain where Sixes stand with them. Suspicion and paranoia lead to hostile, defensive behavior, blaming and instilling fear in others.

TYPE 6
SEEKING GUIDANCE

TYPE ■   WINGS ■   SECURITY POINT ■   STRESS POINT ■

UNHEALTHY

Unbalanced Sixes will try to preserve their security at any cost. They become increasingly anxious, volatile, and fearful of others, while seeking out an even stronger authority figure. At this point, they can become distraught and wildly erratic, leaving them at risk for cults and self-destructive behavior.

It's useful for Sixes to adopt practices that ease mental chatter, allowing them to access their internal sense of where to go and what to do. Rather than consulting others for advice, they can make a habit of consulting themselves first.

WINGS

Six with a Five Wing (6w5): These Sixes may have a scholarly bent and are often drawn to systems of thought, method, or philosophy. They appear more settled and rational.

Six with a Seven Wing (6w7): These Sixes are often interested in exploring and participating, seeking guidance through interaction. They are more outwardly energetic and scattered.

ARROWS

Type Six's Stress Point is the boastful Type Three. When they've had enough of taking one for the team, stressed Sixes draw attention to themselves by showing off.

Type Six's Security Point is the peaceful Type Nine. In safe situations, Sixes trade working hard for daydreaming and lounging. Growth toward their Nine Integration Point allows Sixes to genuinely relax their guard and trust that things will work out.

TYPE SEVEN: SEEKING FREEDOM

Sevens on the Enneagram are motivated by the pursuit of freedom and possibility. This can make them delightful people to be around. They have wide-ranging interests and enjoy trying new things. Even something as simple as a trip to the laundromat can become an adventure through a Seven's eyes. If it weren't for the energy of Sevens in the world, we wouldn't have vacations or parties. They show us all that the world can be a buffet of rich experiences to explore. They bring spontaneity, fun, and a boundless sense of joy to life.

HEALTHY

Healthy Sevens are deeply inspired by all the wonderful things in life. Jacks and Jills of all trades, they're wonderfully productive and accomplished. They often integrate ideas and skills across disciplines, creating surprising hybrids. They excel at brainstorming and planning. Sevens seek to live a life of fulfillment, appreciating every moment they experience in their lives. Balanced Sevens make lemonade out of lemons. They are highly resilient people who are able to find personal freedom even in harrowing circumstances.

AVERAGE

Average Sevens are adventurous and seek to have a wide variety of experiences. Variety and novelty are important to them, and their attempts to experience everything cause them to lose focus. To run away from inner feelings of anxiety and sadness, they can sometimes take on too much, bouncing from one thing to another and not finishing what they start. A life of excess can cause cynicism: "I have or have done all these things, so why am I so unfulfilled?" Self-centered, demanding, and insensitive behavior may leave others frustrated with them.

TYPE 7
SEEKING FREEDOM

TYPE WINGS SECURITY POINT STRESS POINT

UNHEALTHY

Unhealthy Sevens seek to avoid pain at all costs. They run away from all responsibilities and participate in extreme, risky activities in order to seek stimulation. This can lead to erratic, dangerous behavior. Unhealthy Sevens are at risk for addictions, depression, and complete burnout.

Sevens benefit from channeling focus into a small number of streams at a time rather than multitasking. Sevens often find they can be more productive and grounded this way. Practices like mindfulness can also help in bringing truly appreciative attention to the present.

WINGS

Seven with a Six Wing (7w6): With a lighter, more whimsical vibe, these Sevens charm and connect with others easily. They often gravitate to mystical ideas like synchronicity.

Seven with an Eight Wing (7w8): With a more pragmatic approach, these Sevens are not afraid to hustle and get things done. They tend to be ambitious and straightforward.

ARROWS

Type Seven's Stress Point is the critical Type One. When they're drained from being relentlessly positive, Sevens become judgmental of others and themselves.

Type Seven's Security Point is the focused Type Five. In safe situations, Sevens withdraw from the overwhelming stimulations they've surrounded themselves with. Growth toward their Five Integration Point lets Sevens concentrate on the specific projects they care about.

TYPE EIGHT: SEEKING POWER

Eights are motivated by the desire to have power and impact. They take a no-holds-barred approach to life and relish risk. Because of this, they act in ways that have wide-reaching effects. Eights have a palpable energy, what some call "executive presence"—when they walk into a room, people take notice. Supremely self-confident, Eights can often be found in leadership positions, whether in business, family, socially, or other spheres of influence. They are people of action who value results and speak their minds.

HEALTHY

Healthy Eights are openhearted and courageous. They use their commanding presence and strength for good by taking a stand for others who are weaker than them. Balanced Eights are natural protectors, keeping an eye on the people they care about and employing their influence to mentor and uplift. They have high energy, resilience, and determination both physically and psychologically. While driven and powerful, they know when to exercise compassion and restraint.

AVERAGE

Average Eights feel like they need to be sturdy and strong at all times. Hardened, energetic, and savvy, they use their strength and resourceful know-how to take charge of situations and manage resources. They're skilled at starting and maintaining enterprises, whether it is founding a company or taking leadership of their family unit. They can become imposing, getting into others' faces and intimidating or even threatening them in order to get their way. Others may become afraid of them and begin to fight back against their need for control.

UNHEALTHY

Unhealthy Eights will resort to any measures to stay in control, including possible unethical and criminal behavior. At this point, their need

TYPE 8
SEEKING POWER

TYPE   WINGS   SECURITY POINT   STRESS POINT

for power and dominance causes them to act recklessly. Unhealthy Eights can be highly destructive and antisocial.

Eights benefit from paying attention to their energy and dialing back when they are expending more than they need to. It's easier for their true strength to shine when they aren't pushing as hard. Service and relationship building help Eights connect with their own powerful hearts.

WINGS

Eight with a Seven Wing (8w7): Playful and roguish, these Eights live large and express their fiery side. They are outwardly ambitious and value their independence.

Eight with a Nine Wing (8w9): Gentler and steadier, these Eights wield a solid sense of confidence and groundedness. They are often quietly protective.

ARROWS

Type Eight's Stress Point is the detached Type Five. When they're worn from action and exertion, Eights retreat into isolation and strategizing.

Type Eight's Security Point is the nurturing Type Two. In safe situations, Eights show their neediness and lean on their intimates. Growth toward their Two Integration Point leads Eights to connect with the heartfelt caring, love, and generosity beneath their steel.

TYPE NINE: SEEKING HARMONY

Nines on the Enneagram are motivated by the desire for harmony. They are able to see the interconnection between all aspects of life— the wonderful and the difficult, humanity, nature, and the cosmos. Everything is united in a symbiotic whole, as balanced as a symphony. When connected to this truth, Nines feel an abiding inner peace. They bring this sense of serenity into their dealings with the world. They excel at setting people at ease and creating environments where all feel welcome.

HEALTHY

Healthy Nines provide a reassuring, steady presence. Deep connectedness with self and others lets them be a source of calm and quiet strength. A powerful, grounded inner core belies their gentle nature. No one can push a balanced Nine around. Their accepting, nonjudgmental nature makes them wonderful mediators who are able to listen to multiple sides of the story and empathize with differing perspectives. They often rise to leadership because they are so likeable and able to bridge divides.

AVERAGE

While healthy Nines incorporate all sides of life into their sense of inner peace, average Nines feel like they need to avoid conflict and get along with others at all times. Kind and complacent, their harmonious and pleasant nature makes them likeable friends or colleagues. They begin to go along with what others around them want in order to keep the peace, disregarding their own needs and desires. As Nines "check out," they become increasingly oblivious to others and disengaged from the world around them. Extreme passivity and unresponsiveness can cause others to become frustrated with them.

TYPE 9
SEEKING HARMONY

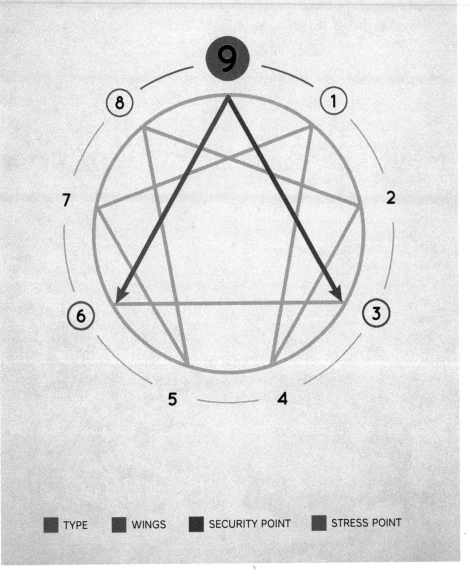

TYPE   WINGS   SECURITY POINT   STRESS POINT

UNHEALTHY

Unhealthy Nines will go to any lengths to avoid conflict and will dissociate to the point of becoming extremely neglectful of themselves and others. At this point, they can become completely numb, confused, and split off from themselves.

Nines benefit from cultivating assertiveness. When they find themselves going along with others, they can ask themselves if they really don't care or if they have an unstated opinion. By paying attention to their own desires, they can identify and pursue the goals that matter to them.

WINGS

Nine with an Eight Wing (9w8): More grounded and embodied, these Nines often exude a sense of laid-back cool. They are stubborn and quicker to anger when provoked.

Nine with a One Wing (9w1): More lofty and idealistic, these Nines often manifest their attention to unity through ideas and imagination. They seem gentler on the surface.

ARROWS

Type Nine's Stress Point is the anxious Type Six. Under stress, Nines shed their typical calm and grow nervous, worrying and scanning the environment for potential threats.

Type Nine's Security Point is the driven Type Three. In safe situations, Nines' desire for attention comes through, and they adopt show-offy behavior. Growth toward their Three Integration Point helps Nines show up in the world in a way that's authentic and valuable.

Toward Self-Discovery

Now that we've covered the nine Enneagram types, as well as the different components that make up the system, maybe one of the types sounds a lot like you, or maybe a few different types sound like possible fits. If that's the case, try them on as you read through the rest of the book, and see which one clicks.

Many people describe feeling a sense of relief when they find their Enneagram type, as they finally have an explanation for why they keep getting caught in the same traps. Through the Enneagram, people not only learn that their personality challenges are not their own fault, but they also get glimpses of their greatest possibilities and gifts. As individuals, we can stop blaming ourselves for our shortcomings and begin to see the beauty in our true selves.

Keep your eyes open and read on with a spirit of self-discovery. As you learn more about your dominant Enneagram type, you'll gain access to a road map of your gifts and challenges. You'll begin to notice when your type's defense mechanisms—the "average type" mindsets that keep you stuck in limiting patterns of behavior—arise. Noticing your reactions and actions as they arise is the first step toward living a free and mindful life. You'll realize that, instead of following the script you're used to, you can make a different choice.

In the next few chapters, we'll take a look at how the different types operate in the workplace, in relationships, and in day-to-day life. You'll gain tools for understanding your own type in context and interacting with others in clear, empathetic, productive ways. Through exploring how the Enneagram can be used in the real world, you'll discover more about yourself and the many ways this system can help you grow.

THE ENNEAGRAM IN PRACTICE

As we just discussed, when you identify your type, the Enneagram gives you a road map—one applicable to your own personal goals and unique life circumstances. The most powerful thing this does is to show you your ultimate potential.

Without actively working on personal growth, many people move through life by merely reacting to the external circumstances around them, simply trying to survive. When in survival mode, it's possible to get small peeks into your talents and gifts, but it's easy to fall back into old patterns of simply making do. By learning your Enneagram type, you get an incredible opportunity to bring your ultimate human potential squarely into your consciousness. This kind of awareness helps motivate you to put the work in to become your best, happiest self. At your healthiest and most present, you have the information needed to make decisions that actively empower you, no matter what your external life circumstances look like.

Once you learn the basics and start practicing, the Enneagram isn't too difficult to interpret. However, with nine different types (not to mention each type's wings and arrows and a bunch of different triads), sometimes it can feel a little confusing, especially at first. To help you get started, let's get to know Julia.

Meet Julia

At 33, Julia has built a life that many would envy. She has a great job, a supportive boyfriend, and the ability to afford her own apartment in a large, expensive city. She lives a 30-minute drive from the suburban area where she grew up. She feels like she has many great options in her life. She is able to enjoy visiting her parents every weekend, but can also live an adventurous life in an urban setting. With a large circle of friends, including coworkers and some schoolmates she grew up with, Julia spends her after-work hours taking advantage of the endless opportunities for entertainment that exist in her city.

Although things are largely going well in Julia's life right now, she also faces some personal challenges. There are a few areas of her life she'd like to improve.

WORK

After working in an administrative role for a few years, Julia was promoted to a managerial position at her branding company about two years ago. Now she manages a team of graphic designers. Julia was frustrated to be "just an administrator" after working hard to get a college degree, but ended up being a natural fit for the role. She's talented at work that requires her to "wear many hats," and handles the complex administrative tasks with ease. Her natural sense of humor and ease with people convinced her bosses to promote her when a managerial position opened up. Julia finds she loves motivating and cheering up her staff. Her optimism and energy translate well to leading a team.

Sometimes, though, Julia feels frustrated by the people she manages. Most of Julia's talented, creative designers are more introverted than she is, and can't keep up with her fast pace. They produce work more slowly than she would like, sometimes missing deadlines she imposes. Many of them prefer to keep their office doors shut, rather than chatting with her. Julia loves her employees, but feels bored easily without the opportunity to work as quickly and do as many things as she'd like. On particularly trying days, Julia finds herself spending work hours searching online for jobs she thinks would be fun and bring in more money, or complaining with her old friends over Facebook messages. She daydreams about the wonderful things a new job would bring, but also feels a bit guilty about considering leaving her work family.

RELATIONSHIPS

Julia met her boyfriend, Miguel, just under a year ago. Despite an active social and dating life, Miguel is the first person Julia has been truly exclusive with since her college boyfriend. Prior to meeting him, she spent a lot of time perusing dating apps and websites and meeting dates at the festivals and bars she frequents. But she never moved beyond casual dating with anyone. She dated numerous interesting people, but she kept wondering if someone better was out there and she was wary to commit. This time is different, though: she really values Miguel's caring, steady, and supportive personality, which has settled her down a bit. And it doesn't hurt that her family and friends love him, too.

But Miguel wants to take their exclusivity further. He dreams of settling down with Julia. A successful professional himself, he knows they can afford to buy a house within commuting distance to their jobs. He has an eye on settling down soon, wanting the commitment of marriage and children in the near future. Julia loves Miguel, but she keeps wondering if he's really "the one." She is anxious about getting tied down by one person when so many other great ones could be out there. While she likes the idea of living in a bigger space, she also wonders if she wants to be permanently tied to the city she's lived in her whole life, when there are so many other fun places out there (places she's already explored on vacation). She also worries that buying a house would limit her career and the companies where she could get hired. And while she enjoys seeking jobs in new cities, she isn't sure how a move would impact her relationship.

WHAT IS JULIA HOPING TO GET FROM THE ENNEAGRAM?

After discovering the Enneagram, Julia hopes this new knowledge of herself and others will help her achieve certain goals. She aims to use the system to improve her work life and relationship in the following ways.

AT WORK

Julia wants to learn how to more effectively work with the creative designers she manages—people whose personalities are mostly very different from hers. She wants to learn to manage them in a way that they can meet their deadlines effectively and stay engaged at work. She wants them to have more fun in the office, too.

Instead of whiling away on social media at work, Julia would like to use her energy and creativity to find and take on more projects that would be interesting to her. She realizes her fun, spontaneous personality means it's difficult for her to finish projects she starts, and she would like structure and support from upper management.

Julia would also like to work toward a promotion at her current company or see what other positions are out there in her field. As discussed previously, she's exploring and applying to jobs in her current city and out of town, wanting to keep her career options open.

IN RELATIONSHIPS

Although Julia loves Miguel, she feels anxious when thinking about making a bigger commitment in her relationship. She'd like to figure out if she should stay with him or move on and try to find a different partner, perhaps one who doesn't want to settle down as quickly.

As Miguel talks more and more about marriage and buying a house, Julia realizes she needs to have an honest conversation with him about her anxieties and see how he feels about her desires.

FOUNDING THINKERS AND MODERN COUNTERPARTS

This wouldn't be much of an Enneagram book without acknowledging the founding thinkers associated with it, as well as their modern counterparts. Here are a few of the heavy hitters:

G. I. Gurdjieff taught the Enneagram as a model of processes, connecting it to sacred dancing. He taught a method of spiritual practice called the Fourth Way, or the "Way of the Sly Man," which involved working on all three Centers at once—the Gut, Heart, and Head Center—while living a regular life engaged in the world. For a modern take on the kinesthetic Enneagram, Brazilian teacher Uranio Paes' trainings incorporate movement work around the nine-pointed symbol. Additionally, Russ Hudson sometimes coleads retreats with Gurdjieff movement teacher Jason Stern.

Oscar Ichazo: Ichazo was the one to synthesize the Enneagram symbol and psychospiritual categorization (even though his ideas of the nine types differ from many modern interpretations). He described each type as an "ego-fixation" that tends to act out a particular sin or imbalance. His creation of the nine types was informed by research on various other spiritual systems. Without Ichazo, there would be no Enneagram of personality.

Claudio Naranjo: Naranjo wrote books that offer a detailed look at the psychological defense mechanisms and patterns of the nine types. He views the types' character structures as different forms of neurosis, and his descriptions highlight their pathological side rather than touching on any positive attributes. Naranjo also developed the idea of "subtypes," describing three instincts and how they interact with each type. Any type can have any dominant instinct. Psychologist Beatrice Chestnut has expanded on Naranjo's work with subtypes.

Don Riso and Russ Hudson: Riso was the first to flesh out the "gray area" of type by writing about nine Levels of Development that describe the type's full potential, from serious mental illness to illuminated presence and awareness. Hudson worked with Riso to integrate a Gurdjieffian emphasis on spiritual practice and balancing the Centers. He remains one of the world's most renowned Enneagram teachers. The Enneagram Institute carries on Riso and Hudson's legacy through workshops and trainings.

Helen Palmer and David Daniels: Palmer's Enneagram books are accessible to a broad audience, describing the Enneagram types as they operate in daily life, including the realms of romance and career. Many authors have followed in her footsteps and written about Enneagram applications ranging from classroom learning to job selection. Palmer, Daniels, and their Enneagram school have fine-tuned the Narrative Tradition approach to the Enneagram—a tradition that dates back to Naranjo, using panels of people who share types or triads to illuminate type patterns in their own words.

A Closer Look

After taking an Enneagram test and closely reading descriptions of the different Enneagram types, Julia identified herself as an Enneagram Type Seven, with a Six Wing. Though we'll learn more details about the types in chapters to follow, we'll focus on what a Seven, and a 7w6, may do in Julia's situation.

ENNEAGRAM TYPE: SEVEN

As an Enneagram Seven, Julia is particularly attuned to seeking out freedom and possibilities. We can see this in the many ways Julia savors and appreciates her life. By choosing life in a large city, she's able to entertain herself with endless things to do every weekend.

Her large circle of friends gives her the chance to experience life with many different people. Her apartment is filled with collections and the curios she loves to buy. By living near but not right next to her family, she gives herself the freedom to live independently with the option of easily spending time with them when she chooses.

Many Seven's strengths come into play in Julia's career. In her previous and current jobs, Julia impressed her bosses with the ability to effortlessly handle several tasks at once. Healthy Sevens are highly productive and able to produce a great deal of work across a breadth of disciplines. She gets enjoyment from her work and knows how to make her job fun. This leads to her interpersonal talent of getting others in her workplace to enjoy themselves, too. Julia always has a smile on her face, even during tougher days at the office, and knows how to motivate employees by getting them to feel great. She throws parties that boost staff morale.

We also see Julia's enjoyment and desire for freedom in her romantic life. Although Julia went several years without a committed relationship, she showed continued motivation and versatility in finding potential suitors through apps, online dating, and the local community. She has shown resilience, another trait in healthy Sevens, by bouncing back when her dating life didn't go as planned. As a partner to Miguel, Julia brings a sense of adventure and excitement to their relationship, introducing spontaneity to his normally settled life.

Julia's challenges are also typical of Sevens in the average range of health. Sevens are natural optimists, but they can become frustrated and cynical when life doesn't work out as positively as they'd dreamed. Julia's life is generally positive, but she becomes frustrated about the aspects of her life that are difficult, such as managing more introverted and slower-paced coworkers and being in a relationship with someone she feels wants to commit too quickly for her.

As a Seven, it can be difficult for Julia to stick with these frustrations long enough to create solutions that work for everyone. Sticking with challenges requires Sevens to process their own frustrations and unhappiness—feelings that are particularly difficult for them to experience. They also can have a hard time experiencing others' negative emotions, such as Julia's employees who are unhappy with her fast way of doing things or her boyfriend being disappointed she hasn't committed.

Instead, it can be easy for Sevens to distract themselves. At work, Julia looks at social media sites for much of the day instead of engaging in productive projects. Going to local events can be a way of distracting herself and seeking stimulation, rather than sources of genuine enjoyment. On a larger scale, Julia engages in "grass is greener" behavior; instead of staying happy with her current life circumstances, she spends a lot of time looking for something different, while not maintaining a connection to her present.

WING: SIX

While all Sevens have the same core motivations and desires, wings create some differences in the "flavoring" of the core Enneagram type. With a Six Wing, Julia remains a Seven, but some of the Enneagram Type Six traits come in to flavor and subtly influence her core Seven traits. Outwardly, she may appear quite different to an impartial observer from a Seven with an Eight Wing.

The Six Wing brings qualities of loyalty and warmth to Julia's personality. She is dependable at her job, having demonstrated commitment by working there for years, and is also loyal to her friends and family. She appreciates the security of her regular salary and the relationships she's developed. The warmth of Type Six adds a sense of softness and charm to the independent and sometimes pushy Type Seven, making it easier for Julia to get along with her colleagues, make friends, and find relationships.

In the more average range of health, Julia is anxious. This can make her appear endearing, but is also makes it even harder to make decisions about her future. She also can feel an increased sense of suspicion around her intimates. When she feels frustrated by her employees and her boyfriend, Julia finds herself questioning whether they're really committed to her. Under stress, this uncertainty is more likely to make Julia act out by moving on to what she believes is the next best thing.

CENTER: THE HEAD CENTER

Type Seven, along with Types Five and Six, is most focused on the Head Center. As a Head Type, Julia is particularly focused on finding clarity around the future. Specifically, Julia would like to make positive decisions in her present to ensure she enjoys her career, has a satisfying love life, and feels happiness in her daily life.

Like all Head Types, Julia is particularly prone to feelings of anxiety and uncertainty around the future. She worries about making the wrong decisions, fearing that they'll leave her trapped in a situation that doesn't work for her. Sometimes, Julia will find herself putting off making decisions out of this fear, choosing her many distractions instead.

SOCIAL STYLE: ASSERTIVE

Along with Types Three and Eight, Type Seven has an assertive way of relating with others. Julia is what you'd describe as a go-getter: she likes to get things done. Her style makes Julia a natural "mover and shaker"; she speaks up in meetings, initiates projects, and asks for what she wants. She's often the person deciding what she and her friends will do on the weekends.

On the downside, it can be difficult for Julia to slow down and reflect, an often-necessary trait when making decisions. She gets impatient with her slower-paced coworkers when they don't move and act as quickly as she would like. Her natural assertiveness sometimes makes it harder for others speak up.

CONFLICT RESOLUTION STYLE: POSITIVE OUTLOOK

Like Twos and Nines, Sevens look on the brighter side of life. Julia's positivity and enthusiasm helps her see the best in her coworkers, friends, and boyfriend, even when they're frustrating her. Her natural good spirits help smooth conflicts over at work and help boost morale with her team on difficult days.

Julia also has a hard time addressing conflicts. She tends to ignore the discontent from her boyfriend and employees, focusing instead on what's going well or distracting herself with other activities. The downside is that, when conflicts go unaddressed, they have the potential to grow bigger, ultimately leading to more frustration and unhappiness.

OBJECT RELATIONS STYLE: FRUSTRATION

Julia's Type Seven joins Ones and Fours in focusing on ideals they want in the world: in Julia's case, she's particularly focused on a world where she has the freedom to buy what she wants and needs, pursue stimulating activities, and have endless friends, while also finding the ultimate job and relationship. Sevens like Julia tend to idealize a lifestyle that will bring them frequent happiness and joy.

The downside is that idealized lives are almost impossible to achieve. This leaves Julia frequently frustrated—with her boyfriend, her job, the place she lives, et cetera—even when much in her life is going well. Instead, she focuses on trying to achieve what she feels she doesn't have.

UNDERSTANDING NUANCES

Here are some factors to pay close attention to when interpreting the Enneagram.

Consider the "Why": Often, people of two different types will take identical actions, but for different reasons. For example, Julia and her friend Lakesha from the marketing department are both eyeing promotions at work. As a Seven, Julia sees a promotion as an exciting opportunity to experience new kinds of work, to bring variety into her professional life. Lakesha, a Three, sees a promotion as a way to advance her standing, reach a long-desired professional goal, and feel like a valuable, worthy contributor in her workplace.

Triad Look-Alikes: Types that share a triadic grouping on the Enneagram have attributes in common. For instance, an energetic go-getter might be any of the Assertive Types, while a person who insists on keeping conflict resolution civil and detached is likely one of the Competency Types. When they share a style of being in the world, it can be hard to tell types apart. Luckily, there are four sets of triads to take into account. If you have a good sense that someone is in one triad, take a look at the other triadic groupings to see which ones fit best, and narrow down type possibilities from there.

Movement Along the Arrows: Especially when you're typing family members, who you see at their most uninhibited, it's easy to confuse the manifestations of their Security Point for their core type. For instance, a Six will often daydream and seek comfort around intimates in a way that resembles a Nine. Stress Points are also a factor to consider, with many of us acting on stress multiple times a day. Under major stress, someone can move to their Stress Point type for years. To differentiate core type from movement along the arrows, look for consistent threads of behavior and preoccupation across all areas and eras of a person's life.

Practical Applications

Julia has spent time reading and reflecting about her Enneagram type. She has some solid guesses about the types of her partner and colleagues as well. Now she's ready to apply the Enneagram toward her goals.

AT WORK

Julia wants to understand where her colleagues are coming from and create an effective balance between their different work styles. As a Seven, she recognizes that she lives life at a fast pace. If she has one creative idea, it's not long before her focus has shifted to another. She actively enjoys having multiple projects on the go. This is not the case for the designers she manages. She's identified many of them as Withdrawn Types (Types Four, Five, and Nine), predominantly Fours. When she's in a generous mood, she describes her team to Miguel as "liking to take their time," and when she's frustrated, she complains to him about the team's disconnect with her time management efforts. Why can't they come up with ideas on the spot, the way she does? Why do they approach deadlines as if they were just suggestions? Why are they all so quiet?

After learning more about the Withdrawn Types she works with, Julia recognizes that their minds operate differently than hers. They need time to think their concepts through before pursuing them, and the quiet that pervades the office comes from their deep concentration. Rather than pushing them to work more quickly or making the office more "fun," she will be a more effective manager if she gives them the space they need—to think and to work.

In terms of deadlines, she recognizes that the Fours on her team are motivated by the drive to be individuals, connected to their personal subjectivity. Some of them are resistant when she imposes a uniform structure on their work without recognizing the individuality and unique needs of their projects. Realizing this, Julia starts to bring a more personal touch to her meetings with her Type Four designers.

They come to a consensus around the needs of the client and the project and agree on a deadline. Julia listens with greater attention to the designers' creative needs and concerns. This acknowledgment makes it easier for the designers to follow Julia's structure and understand its importance.

In her own quest to trade workplace distraction for engagement in more interesting projects, Julia acknowledges that focus will help. It's easy and fun to check her Facebook feed during downtime, but in the long term, she feels like she's wasted a lot of time and recognizes that it would be more rewarding to try out a new task. She uses her strength of generating possibilities to brainstorm projects that she might like to try on the job. Knowing that a supporter will help her focus, she meets with her friend Lakesha to talk through the list together. One option that they decide is both reasonable and exciting involves approaching a senior colleague about participating in the Women's Leadership Committee. This colleague is stepping down from her role as the committee's co-organizer and looking for a replacement. Julia asks the remaining co-organizer if she is willing to mentor her, and the co-organizer accepts. Julia now has an appealing new role and a supporter to help keep her structured. As she connects with the women on the Leadership Committee, many of whom have seniority in her field, she asks them questions about their roles and responsibilities. Recognizing her tendency to make quick decisions, she challenges herself to be more deliberate in exploring different career possibilities for herself. She plans to keep looking into future work options while committing to her current role and new responsibility for the time being. She will aim to find something that will provide both variety and long-term reward.

IN RELATIONSHIPS

Before learning about the Enneagram, Julia had no idea how many of her actions were driven by anxiety. Now, she realizes that her fear is a driving force behind her efforts to escape from commitment with Miguel. It's not that her relationship is particularly problematic. She would be nervous about committing to *any* relationship. The next time Miguel brings up his house-and-marriage goals, she decides that she owes him a conversation.

She has identified Miguel as a Two on the Enneagram, a connection-oriented romantic. He wants her to commit in order to be assured that she loves him. The more he pushes her, the more confined she feels, and the more she questions whether she wants to stay with him. But when they aren't letting their insecurities get in the way, they have a great relationship. They enjoy cooking and going to festivals together, watching TV shows, and discussing ideas. They are affectionate and supportive of each other's goals. She realizes that she can't entirely blame him for their relationship disconnect. By distracting herself with activities that don't involve him and hiding her interest in jobs outside the city, she's been treating him as a threat to avoid rather than as a teammate.

As a Heart Triad type, Miguel responds to the language of feelings. Despite her anxiety about doing so, Julia opens up to him about her recent emotions. She tells him that, while she loves him very much, she's been feeling nervous about the many levels of commitment that he wants from her. She isn't sure if she wants to stay in the area indefinitely, or have kids, and she's terrified by the thought of committing to a marriage, house, and family all at once. She understands that he wants a commitment from her, and she's wondering if he would be willing to take things more slowly.

To her relief, Miguel wraps her in a big hug. He, too, hadn't realized the extent of her anxiety. He had assumed that a home and family were goals she aspired toward as clearly as he did, and that her doubts came from not loving him enough. He's reassured by her explanation of how much she does love him, and while he'd like to build a life together, he is open to exploring different lifestyle options with her. They decide to compromise and try out living together by renting a house on the outskirts of the city, rather than buying property immediately. They set a flexible timeline with goals for their work lives and their life together. They also commit to a weekly date night. Julia will use her gift for coming up with activities that are fun and stimulating, and their dates will give Miguel the opportunity to connect with his partner and demonstrate their caring for each other.

IN DAILY LIFE

Julia has several framed prints in her apartment that feature inspirational messages. "Dance like no one is watching." "Live the life you've dreamed of!" "Don't worry, be happy!" Setting down her Enneagram book, she laughs at the typical Type Seven philosophy reflected all over her walls. She has no problem keeping possibility and positivity in mind, but maybe her life could use a new slogan.

She orders a pretty print that says, "Take time to smell the roses." It's a reminder of her intention to live deliberately rather than letting her own impatience and stimulation seeking get in the way of her real desires. It's also an acknowledgment that others in her life need time and space. For Julia, as well, these things are useful. She's tried having a daily meditation practice before as a way to connect with herself, but she hasn't maintained it. She starts setting her alarm a half hour early every morning to create structure for meditation. Sitting on the mat, being mindful of her thoughts and feelings as they arise, is initially a dull and anxiety-producing process. As weeks go by, she finds her thoughts calming down. She begins to have more clarity about the choices that truly speak to her. She feels proud of her ability to take time for herself and to commit to a practice that supports her.

When planning her move with Miguel, she realizes she has a lot of clutter in her apartment that she doesn't really need. She spends a few days filling donation bags with old clothes and sentimental items that she hadn't necessarily wanted to get rid of, but which she realizes no longer bring her genuine joy. The next time she's tempted to buy something extra at the store, she finds herself being mindful of the impulse and asking herself whether it's an item she will value or another momentary distraction.

SPIRITUAL APPLICATION
OF THE ENNEAGRAM

The Enneagram is a wonderful personality typology. But using it solely from this perspective keeps us from gaining the full benefit the system can bring. It makes a great foundation for, or addition to, a spiritual practice. No matter your worldview or spiritual inclination, the Enneagram brings insights that complement your beliefs. This versatility is not surprising for a system with origins that blend Sufism (Islamic mysticism), mystical Judaism and Christianity, esoteric philosophy, and modern psychology.

Through its unifying circle, the Enneagram shows that all of us are connected. But it truly enhances our spiritual practice by highlighting our differences. Religions and spiritual practices often prescribe a specific path for growth. Even so, the reality is that we all have different needs. A spiritual practice that works well for a Five may be very different than what supports an Eight. For example, some of us benefit profoundly from reflection or meditation, while others get more deeply in touch with a sense of something greater through service or direct action. The Enneagram allows us to celebrate our differences and customize a personal plan for spiritual growth.

Your Enneagram type gives you direction to get in touch with your true self. Even though we all have a core personality type, everyone is really much more than their personality. The spiritual path gives you the opportunity to wake up to a deeper reality, and the Enneagram helps by showing you which patterns of thinking and behavior take you away from that reality. The key to waking up is to "catch ourselves in the act," as Riso and Hudson call it: to be aware of our thoughts and emotions as we experience them. This mindfulness allows you to catch glimpses of your true, observing self, operating beneath your habitual psychological patterns. With time, these glimpses increase, giving deeper and fuller contact with your true nature.

To learn more about the spiritual roots and applications of the Enneagram, check out the Spiritual Growth portion of the Resources section.

Becoming Your Whole Self

With an understanding of her Enneagram type and its meaning, Julia can approach life from a clearer perspective than she did before. She has learned that her usual ways of making decisions stem from bias in favor of the next exciting thing. What she really wants is freedom and joy, but these are deeper qualities than the momentary stimulation she substitutes for them. With the Enneagram in mind, she has a map for making life choices that satisfy her true needs.

Learning about her Type Seven patterns has taught her to be mindful of her daily habits. She now knows how easily she gets distracted, and how often she abandons potentially promising pursuits the moment they stop feeling stimulating or start feeling like commitment. When she catches herself falling into any of these habits (which she does, several times a day), she asks herself, "Will this *really* make me happy?" If the answer is "no," she considers her choice more carefully. Sometimes she takes the action anyway, but now she is more mindful of consequences. Sometimes she chooses to do something different, and she is often satisfied with the results of these different choices.

Julia also realizes that the people in her life are so different from her that the Golden Rule doesn't always apply. The team of designers she manages doesn't urgently need to have more fun; what they want is time and space for their creative processes to unfold. Her boyfriend isn't trying to trap her; he's trying to connect more deeply and know that he is loved. With the Enneagram as a map, she seeks to understand others' viewpoints and needs rather than assuming that they share hers.

Julia is at a point in her life where she has a lot of decisions to make. With the help of the Enneagram, she will make them with her best self in mind.

In this chapter, we took a deep dive into how one person applied the Enneagram in her life. In the next chapter, we'll take a closer look at how the Enneagram can be applied in a professional context.

THE
ENNEAGRAM
AT WORK

Many companies make use of the Enneagram to find ways
to create harmony among employees—people who are all
working toward the same goal, but may have vastly different
ways of getting there. Individuals can also use the Enneagram
to find a good career fit, help set professional goals, and
advance in their chosen vocation. You may have picked up
this book because you want guidance in your own career
journey, or because you want to learn to communicate and
get along with coworkers who don't see eye-to-eye with you.
This chapter can help. In the next few pages, we'll review how
each Enneagram type functions in a work environment, how
each type may approach a career, and how you can avoid
your type's common pitfalls on the job.

Solving Problems at Work

The Enneagram is a popular way for businesses to help their teams understand each other and improve their performance and communication. It's a useful tool for mediating disputes and resolving interpersonal conflicts on the job.

After learning about the nine types, Julia, an Enneagram Type Seven, started applying her new knowledge to her job of managing a team of graphic designers at a branding firm. She had her colleagues take an Enneagram type assessment, and they now have a common language to talk about each other's personalities and viewpoints. Let's take a look at a scenario where the Enneagram helped solve a problem involving a diverse group of people in Julia's workplace.

Bob is a repeat client of the firm where Julia works. He has contracted with the company to rebrand his business, including a new logo and marketing strategy. Exacting and critical, he has many specifications for the project. Having worked with Bob before, Julia believes him to be a Type One.

Kevin, a Type Four, is the designer in charge of visual branding for Bob's company. He completed a logo and portfolio of visual material for the rebranding project, but Bob is dissatisfied with Kevin's colorful, free-form designs. He wants the whole portfolio redesigned, and he has many specific changes that he would like Kevin to make. Being a One, he has high expectations and desires a brand identity that gets all the details right. He tells Julia that he wants the new portfolio within a set timeline, and says that if it isn't up to his standards, he will not work with the company in the future. As a Seven, Julia wants to keep interactions optimistic—and she does not want to lose a valuable client. She assures Bob that Kevin will give him what he wants.

Kevin, however, says the timeline is unrealistic. It's just too tight for him to redesign all the material required. Julia does not have a background in graphic design, and her knowledge of the field comes from working with designers rather than from firsthand experience. She doesn't understand why a redesign can't be done quickly.

Kevin explains that Bob's expected timeline will not result in the powerful visual brand identity his company desires. At best, it will result in some slapdash materials that don't reflect the quality the branding firm is known for. As a Four, Kevin takes the creative process seriously and values producing well-developed and eye-catching work. Kevin needs more time to come up with new concepts that will fit Bob's precise specifications and still stand out in the market.

Lakesha, who heads the marketing department, is also advocating quick turnaround. She needs to have the visual branding finished in order for her department to complete the marketing strategy for Bob's company and have it ready for an upcoming launch party. As a Three on the Enneagram, she wants the branding firm to put their best foot forward, and she sees satisfying the client as part of that.

Julia feels caught between Kevin's request for more time, and Bob and Lakesha's requests for more speed. She expresses her frustration to Lakesha—who has more design knowledge than Julia—and they decide to problem solve together. When she hears about the level of changes that Bob wants Kevin to make to the visual branding portfolio, Lakesha agrees that the timeline is unrealistic. Julia is resistant at first. After all, managing interactions with designers is her job, and she wants to make the customer happy. When Lakesha suggests negotiating a compromise with Bob, Julia realizes that she has some workable ideas (and strategies to deliver them) that will please both Bob and Kevin.

Julia contacts Bob and tells him that she respects the integrity of his vision for his company (a strong value for Bob as a One), and her branding firm is committed to representing this vision in the world. She uses her Type Seven strength of positivity to emphasize the advantages of Kevin's design, and explains that, in order to get the new portfolio completed in time, Bob will need to compromise on some of the changes he wants. She speaks to the effort Kevin is putting in and the high standards of the firm's design process. Bob is still grumpy, but Julia's upbeat manner and understanding of his values assuage him somewhat. He is willing to compromise on certain aspects of the redesign, though not on the timeline.

Julia and Lakesha talk to Kevin together about the compromises Bob is willing to make. Kevin is relieved that, with a less intensive redesign, the timeline is closer to being workable. Lakesha proposes a structured plan for completing the project on time, and Julia expresses full confidence in his work. With Julia motivating him, Kevin is able to complete the redesigned logo and portfolio, and Lakesha's team moves ahead with the marketing strategy.

Ultimately, Bob feels that his company's rebrand is in good hands because Julia used honesty and integrity when dealing with him. Kevin feels like his creative process has been respected. Lakesha is happy to have achieved her client's goal of a successful launch, and kept the firm's good standing in Bob's eyes. Julia is relieved that everyone involved with the redesign conflict is satisfied and on good terms. Thanks to the Enneagram, their needs and viewpoints have all been heard. They can move on to the next project harmoniously, without any lingering tension.

Enneagram Types on the Job

When applying the Enneagram to a professional setting, it's helpful to look at the types of the people you work with as well as your own type. Each personality has distinctive ways of approaching work. When you can understand where your colleagues are coming from, as Julia and her team did, you can solve complex problems more readily. The profiles given next present the gifts and challenges each type brings to a job, as well as tips for putting their best foot forward in the workplace.

TYPE ONE: THE MISSION-DRIVEN PERFECTIONIST

Ones are largely motivated by their principles and a desire for goodness. This may result in integrity and conscientiousness or in a tendency to be critical.

Strengths: Ones bring integrity and commitment to their work. Responsible and conscientious, they excel at making sure things are done right. They contribute an eye for detail and are willing to go the extra mile. At their best, Ones' professional lives exemplify the term "mission-driven." They are often the people who set standards for their team.

Challenges: Ones struggle with perfectionism, both inward and outward. It can be a challenge for Ones not to expect too much from themselves, or from the people they work with. They may become critical and frazzled. They may also get stressed by putting in more effort than others, trying to ensure quality control by taking on extra work.

Tips: Ones can be their best selves at work by cultivating a stance of acceptance toward workplace realities. There are imperfect aspects to every workplace, and these can be managed more effectively when Ones relax a little. Recognizing others' efforts will help Ones see how much their colleagues care, and trusting this will lighten their load. Bonding with coworkers and allowing themselves to have fun will make their mission a lot more enjoyable.

TYPE TWO: THE EMPATHETIC CONNECTOR

Twos are real people persons, motivated by the desire to build loving, mutually nurturing relationships. In the workplace, their striving to connect can be both a boon and a burden.

Strengths: Empathetic, emotionally intelligent Twos excel at bringing a personal touch to their work. Many are gifted at cultivating relationships with clients and colleagues. They go the extra mile to show the people they work with how much they mean to them, and are quick to lend a hand when needed. Valuable mentors and networkers, Twos can contribute greatly to the cohesion of their team.

Challenges: Twos can focus so much on others' needs that they lose touch with their own. Often comfortable in support roles, they may put in extra work behind the scenes and feel resentful when their contributions go unacknowledged. They may become overbearing in their efforts to help, or be distracted from tasks and goals by interpersonal interaction.

Tips: Twos can be their best selves at work by being attentive to their own needs before committing to help. It can be easy for Twos to volunteer for things, or to step in to fill a perceived need, without checking in with their time and energy. Being centered in themselves at work will ensure Twos don't overcommit. Further, cultivating balanced self-care in general will help Twos excel on the job. It's also helpful for Twos to cultivate interests and projects at work that don't directly involve people.

TYPE THREE: THE ADAPTABLE PERFORMER

Threes are motivated by success and recognition. They tend to be self-assured and adaptable at work, at the risk of valuing image over substance. In the workplace, these characteristics lend themselves to both positives and negatives.

Strengths: Adaptable Threes are able to quickly assess others' desires and make changes accordingly, creating a natural affinity for marketing and presentation in multiple capacities. At work, Threes are dedicated and efficient. They focus on achieving goals and are motivated by tasks and recognition. At their best, they bring their true selves to their work and excel at inspiring others.

Challenges: Stressed Threes may be tempted to take shortcuts or overwork to get results. They may present an image of high achievement, while overlooking less visible yet equally important aspects of the job. Threes can also be resistant to delegating because they believe they will do a better job with the work than their colleagues. Burnout is possible under high pressure.

Tips: To bring out their best at work, it's useful for Threes to learn to recognize when they are overworking, and create breaks for themselves. Delegating can stress Threes in the short term, but ultimately prove helpful. Honoring their own integrity is also important for this type. Threes benefit from paying attention to their own interests and choose work that is in line with these, rather than seeking to do whatever will get the highest recognition.

TYPE FOUR: THE COMPASSIONATE CREATOR

Motivated by desires to know and express themselves, Fours bring creativity and sensitivity to their work, with the danger of being overly emotional.

Strengths: Expressive Fours bring a creative touch to their work. They may create unique products or distinctive designs, drawing inspiration from their emotions and imagination. High-functioning Fours can attune to the emotions of their clients or colleagues and empathize with their deepest challenges. Fours bring emotional intelligence to their teams, along with a willingness to identify and face problems.

Challenges: The daily grind of work can be a struggle for Fours to sustain. When under stress or emotionally provoked, they may retreat and look to process their feelings before they are able to move on and be productive. Their emotional outbursts and touch-iness can create workplace drama. Four may also procrastinate when nervous about projects.

Tips: To bring their gifts out at work, Fours benefit from implementing structure and regularity. Deadlines and schedules are useful, and checking in regularly with colleagues helps hold them accountable. When their sensitivities or negative emotions are provoked, they might benefit from taking a time-limited break and engaging their body in a way that grounds them in reality, such as taking a short walk.

TYPE FIVE: THE INNOVATIVE SPECIALIST

In search of clarity and masterful knowledge, Fives are keenly perceptive and innovative, seeing connections overlooked by others and sometimes neglecting the interpersonal sphere.

Strengths: Gifted with curiosity and focus, Fives make natural experts. Their analytical minds allow them to take in vast amounts of information, make new connections, and innovate. Fives are often the experts or specialists on their team, accumulating and applying encyclopedic knowledge. High-functioning Fives bring an objectivity and eye for detail that allow for perceptive problem solving.

Challenges: Dealing with people does not come naturally to reserved Fives. They are easily overwhelmed by what they perceive as others' demands, and may retreat from interaction. Alternately, they may only want to talk about specific interests. These behaviors can make them seem unavailable or uncaring to colleagues, challenging team morale and cohesion.

Tips: Fives can be their best selves at work by becoming part of a support network, even in small ways. They benefit from learning how to connect with others without becoming overwhelmed. Fives might set a goal of talking every week at the meeting, or going to lunch with a group of coworkers. Building connections makes Fives feel more appreciated and less isolated and thus more likely to make valuable, creative contributions.

TYPE SIX: THE COMMITTED EGALITARIAN

Sixes are the Enneagram's team-builders, placing huge value on collaboration and interconnection. Their tendency to be skeptical leads to masterful troubleshooting but also, sometimes, paranoia.

Strengths: Naturally collaborative, Sixes lead from within a group, inspiring equality and collegiality. Once committed to a venture, they put in the hard work to see it through. They are often the troubleshooters of the team, anticipating risks and coming up with solutions in advance. High-functioning Sixes are courageous advocates for people and causes they care about.

Challenges: Sixes worry about negative outcomes and focus on how to avoid them. They may get caught up in worry at work and get sidetracked from the job that needs to get done. This can result in them putting in a lot of effort without necessarily fulfilling their goals. Stressed Sixes may complain on the job and raise others' suspicions about threats that may not be accurate.

Tips: To bring out their best selves at work, Sixes benefit from thinking about how to optimize their chances of success, rather than minimize their chances of failure. They can use their natural gift for support-seeking to set up networks of peers who will motivate each other and keep each other on task. When opportunities to use their gifts present themselves, Sixes benefit from facing any nervousness head-on and embracing the chance to grow and shine.

TYPE SEVEN: THE ENERGETIC EXPLORER

Freedom, possibility, and adventure motivate Sevens in their lives and work. Their drive toward novelty can bring both innovation and distraction.

Strengths: Sevens bring joy and liveliness to their work. Clients and colleagues often love their sense of fun and creative ideas. Quick moving and engaging, they may be proficient in several areas, which they're able to combine in exciting ways. At their best, their positivity keeps them resilient. If one thing doesn't work out, they're willing to try another.

Challenges: New possibilities catch a Seven's attention easily. They may begin one project and then get distracted by another. Sometimes they take on so many responsibilities that they are unable to fulfill their obligations to all of them. Stressed Sevens may present an upbeat facade, telling tales of exciting futures while evading present problems.

Tips: Sevens can bring out their best at work by cultivating focus. Their challenge is to learn when to commit to the enterprise at hand rather than pursue the next big thing. It can help for Sevens to set schedules for themselves for important projects while allowing space for their other ideas to develop. For instance, they could commit to a month of working toward one deadline, while keeping a notebook or file of potential projects for the future.

TYPE EIGHT: THE IMPACTFUL DOER

People of action, Eights have a tendency to wind up in leadership positions. However, their risk-taking nature can be equal parts exhilarating and unnerving in the workplace.

Strengths: Street-smart Eights have a knack for making things happen. Commanding a room comes naturally to them. Due to their powerful presence and interest in having a big impact, they often seek out leadership positions on a team. They are people of action, unafraid to make decisions. High-functioning Eights exhibit immense courage, and are able to empower others as well as themselves.

Challenges: Eights don't always realize how strongly they come off to others, and may unwittingly intimidate people. When stressed, they can act aggressively and become more hardheaded than compassionate, making harsh decisions and getting into fights. They may find their work relationships strained because colleagues are afraid of them.

Tips: At work, Eights can be their best selves by noticing how much energy they're putting into interactions, and learning when to dial it down. "Lowering the volume" will create a more harmonious, pleasant work environment. Working on emotional intelligence is also helpful. A little bit of gentleness and compassion goes a long way, allowing Eights to bring out their natural strengths of protectiveness and merciful leadership.

TYPE NINE: THE EASYGOING MEDIATOR

Harmony-seekers, Nines on the Enneagram are able to see that we're all connected. Their desire for peace may result in serenity or passivity in their workplace dealings.

Strengths: These patient personalities are gifted at seeing both sides of an issue and guiding others toward consensus. Because of these talents, Nines are able to connect with others easily. Even in fraught situations, high-functioning Nines have a knack for putting people at ease. They create relaxing work environments—ones where everyone feels comfortable and included.

Challenges: Nines have a slow, gentle, accommodating approach that can result in them not speaking their minds or sharing their ideas. They can fly under the radar at work, resulting in their valuable creativity going unused. Nines may even get into trouble by refusing to take a stand. When stressed, they may stubbornly refuse to participate.

Tips: Nines can be their best selves at work by learning to access their own strong will and make tough decisions. They benefit from practicing assertiveness, and gaining comfort with actions that may rock the boat but move their work ahead. Taking the lead and allowing themselves to be visible at times are both beneficial for Nines. So is taking action on endeavors they have always wanted to do but are nervous about or procrastinating on.

COMMUNICATING WITH COLLEAGUES

Many conflicts at work arise from differing communication styles. Our most popular workshop, *Communication Styles for Success*, introduces the Enneagram's social styles as a way of understanding how our colleagues prefer to convey and receive information. When you use the social styles to communicate, you'll have an easier time speaking your coworkers' language and getting your point across effectively.

The Assertive Types (Three, Seven, and Eight) are Initiators at work. They relish taking on challenges and making quick decisions. Initiators are often the first ones to speak up, employing an energetic, direct style and "thinking aloud." When working with Initiators, be direct and confident with your communication. These colleagues appreciate a forthright perspective and respect those who are willing to debate with them.

The Compliant Types (One, Two, and Six) are Cooperators at work. Their idealistic, naturally collaborative style means they often take on support roles; they focus on drawing out others' participation or following a set of responsibilities. It's helpful to ask Cooperators for their own opinions, which they may not think to volunteer on their own. They benefit from being acknowledged and appreciated for the work they contribute.

The Withdrawn Types (Four, Five, and Nine) are Soloists at work. They take a strategic, long-range perspective and often prefer to work independently. Soloists are innovative and think their ideas through before speaking. When you're working with Soloists, it helps to alert them to upcoming discussions and give them time to prepare their comments, such as by sending the agenda for a meeting out beforehand. Encourage them to contribute in a way that makes space for them to collect their thoughts rather than pushing for immediate input.

Common Careers for the Enneagram Types

There are no direct correlations between Enneagram types and jobs, but the innate interests and preferences of each type mean they gravitate toward certain ways of working. In this section, we'll take note of industries where we commonly see specific Enneagram types. Notice that many industries overlap and many types excel in them. Also, be aware that these are general observations and trends. You can find any type working in any field successfully, thriving by tailoring the job to their personality. If you're looking for a career launch or transition, you might find professions correlated with your type to be good fits for you. Other important factors to consider when selecting a career include your hobbies, talents, and personal interests.

TYPE ONE

Ones are often drawn to professions that strongly involve their sense of personal ethics, mission, and purpose, such as:

▶ **The Legal System:** Ones are frequently lawyers, judges, or paralegals who work to reform rules and standards to bring justice to the world.

▶ **Education:** We see Ones who are principals, academic administrators, and teachers. These professions allow Ones to imbue future generations with values.

▶ **Nonprofits and Social Justice:** Ones are often involved in activism and social justice, areas they believe in strongly. We often see Ones doing macro-level work in these organizations, where their sense of detail and big-picture rules and ideals benefit the organizations.

- **Politics:** The same strong sense of social justice and principles often calls Ones to work in policy, government positions, or run for office themselves.

- **Religious Occupations:** As religious clergy or employees in a religious institution, many Ones find a career path in line with their values, where they can share their sense of mission with a larger community.

- **Health Professionals:** Type One doctors, nutritionists, and other health industry professionals are drawn to the profession's sense of ethics, attentiveness to details, and high standards.

Famous Ones in these occupations include Al Gore and Joan of Arc.

It's also common to see Ones in professions that make use of their strong organizational skills and analytical thinking.

- **Scientific Professions:** Ones often work as scientists, engineers, and architects. Strong attention to detail, combined with high standards and goals, makes Ones interested and excellent in these professions.

- **Tax Professionals:** Ones make wonderful accountants, tax preparers, and auditors, where they can work carefully and adhere to given standards.

- **The Financial Industry:** Ones excel in banking, the mortgage industry, and other positions in finance that require a careful attention to detail.

- **Home Organization:** Ones can be excellent general contractors and professional organizers, ensuring the work is done thoroughly and to high standards and quality.

- **Quality Assurance:** Strong attention to detail makes Ones great editors and inspectors, among other positions that require a similar knack for finding errors.

- **Administrative Professionals:** Ones can apply their detail-oriented outlook to positions in administration, administrative support, and executive assistance.

Famous Ones in these occupations include Martha Stewart and Tom Brokaw.

TYPE TWO

Twos are frequently attracted to people- and service-oriented professions where they provide direct support and care to others.

- **Healthcare Industry:** Positions on the front lines of care—nurses, occupational therapists, and doctors—are often staffed by Twos—people who love giving a personal touch and warm care to their patients.

- **Therapeutic Professionals:** Many Twos work as psychologists, therapists, social workers, speech language pathologists, and personal coaches, where they can use their attunement to people and relationships to help others.

- **Education and Child Development:** Special education teacher, postsecondary student services professional, career counselor, educator, and childcare worker are great choices for Twos, who can help students develop intellectual curiosity combined with personal support.

- **Hospitality:** The food service and hospitality industries staff many Twos, who can provide direct support, service, and enjoyment in these roles.

- **Administrative Support:** Front-facing support positions, such as receptionists and executive assistants, allow Twos to provide excellent service and relationally oriented help.

Famous Twos in these occupations include Richard Simmons and Florence Nightingale.

We also see Twos working in professions that allow them to directly manage and support the relationships between other people:

- **Business Managers:** Twos make excellent managers and supervisors in a business or corporate environment, where they can help manage relationships between teams or between different levels of management.

- **Ministry:** Twos do well as ministers and in other religious positions that involve direct contact and managing relationships with congregations.

- **Relationship Counselors:** Twos are often excellent in professions such as couples counselor, family therapist, business coach, or relationship coach, where they can help others communicate and get along with each other.

- **Professional Networker:** Positions like volunteer coordinator, professional recruitment, or any office position that involves introducing and connecting professionals allow Twos to utilize their strengths of connecting others.

- **Customer Service:** Working in direct customer service allows Twos to use their strength of managing relationships, while working to keep customers and employees happy.

Famous Twos in these occupations include Bishop Desmond Tutu and Byron Katie.

TYPE THREE

Threes are often drawn to positions that involve high visibility and are goal-oriented, with a ladder of achievement they can climb to succeed.

- **Business Professionals:** Many Threes are successful at all levels of business, ranging from office staff all the way to independent consultants and executives. Business environments give Threes the structure to create outstanding, successful work.

- **High-Visibility Professions:** It's common to see Threes in high-profile occupations that also support others, such as doctors, lawyers, and dentists. Threes are able to meet measurable goals of success in these professions, while helping others.

- **Politics:** A sense of wanting to help others, combined with the ability to know what it takes to win, gives many Threes an interest in running for office, running political campaigns, and other related positions.

- **Communications:** High-visibility mass communication positions, such as those in broadcast and radio journalism, public affairs, newspaper reporting, and social media, fit the Three's polished image and assertive, goal-oriented mindset.

- **Marketing and Sales:** Positions in marketing and sales departments, as well as independent positions like real estate agents, allow Threes to perform and sell, and to use their sense of polish to meet goals and sell quality products.

- **Human Resource Professionals:** Many Threes end up combining their strong business sense with a desire to support other professionals in the HR department.

- **Performers, Entertainers, and Athletes:** An interest in entertaining others and knowing how to meet goals and succeed often make Threes polished stars in the entertainment and performance industries, and extremely successful athletes.

Famous Threes in these occupations include Mitt Romney and Taylor Swift.

Other Threes bring their strong sense of knowing how to polish, support, and motivate others into various forms of success.

- **Public Relations:** Threes are often successfully employed as agents, spokespeople, and public relations managers who use their image awareness to present companies and individuals in ways that create success.

- **Coaches:** Threes make excellent personal and business coaches, and are particularly good at inspiring people to set goals and present their best, most authentic selves to succeed in their chosen fields.

- **Image Consultant:** Threes know how to create the polish necessary to help others succeed, and make excellent suggestions in areas like personal grooming, polished manners, and high-impact speaking.

- **Motivational Speaker:** Threes can be wonderful motivational speakers who inspire others to go forth and achieve their own dreams.

- **Athletic Support Professional:** Athletic coaches, personal trainers, sports medicine doctors, and other careers in sports and fitness give Threes a place to help teams and individuals meet their athletic goals.

Famous Threes in these occupations include motivational speaker Tony Robbins and fashionista Stacy London.

TYPE FOUR

Fours are often found in positions that allow for creativity and self-expression, with some flexibility to work on their own timeline.

- **Creative Performers:** Fours are particularly interested in developing their own creative expression through creative professions, such as actors, artists, musicians, and dancers.

- **Writers and Researchers:** Fours with talent in writing, or intellectual pursuits, bring polish, creativity, and self-motivation as copywriters, novelists and memoir writers, curriculum developers, researchers, and journalists.

- **Designers:** Fours can bring their orientation to depth and beauty as website and graphic designers, animators, fashion designers, interior decorators, or landscapers.

- **Marketing and Recruiting:** Often, Fours do wonderful work in the marketing or staff recruitment departments in businesses, as they add their creativity to sales, and are often highly personally attuned to who will fit a particular corporate role.

- **Entrepreneurs:** Although Fours succeed in traditional corporate positions, many prefer the creative flexibility and independence that comes from freelancing, consulting, founding a business, or combining part-time positions.

Famous Fours in these occupations include Johnny Depp and Anne Rice.

Other Fours are drawn to careers with an interest in supporting people and relationships and adding a personal touch.

- **Directors and Managers:** Fours bring sensitivity and caring to managing others in business, and a personal touch to leadership positions. Often, but not always, they direct creatively oriented businesses.

- **Teachers:** Fours make attentive and caring teachers of all age groups, and are particularly seen teaching creative professions in which they excel.

- **Therapeutic Professionals:** The ability to listen attentively to others' personal stories and a desire to support others in working through their feelings make Fours excellent therapists and coaches.

- **Healing Practitioners:** Fours are seen in many healing roles, including traditional medical professions (to which they may bring a holistic approach), instructing yoga, and self-created healing roles that combine modalities.

- **Humanitarian Work and Activism:** Strong feelings often make Fours passionate about causes. They can be seen working in various roles in nonprofits, social justice, activism, and other forms of personal support for what they believe in.

Famous Fours in these occupations include Don Riso (founder of The Enneagram Institute) and Jackie Kennedy Onassis.

OTHER FACTORS TO CONSIDER

The Wings: Your type's wing may also influence your career choice and leadership style at work. For example, a Five with a Four Wing may be more drawn to bringing creative and holistic analysis to their work, and working independently. A Five with a Six Wing may be more drawn to fine-tuned technical or financial analysis in their profession, and work in an independent niche in a larger team.

The Arrows: Recall that each type has an arrow to two other types: their Stress Point and Security Point. You may enjoy elements of careers and working styles types that your arrows enjoy. A One, for example, may want to bring creative freedom into their work from Type Four, or spontaneity, fun, and possibilities from Type Seven.

Your Personal Interests and Abilities: As you've seen, there is a wide variety of careers on each type's list—and many people succeed in type atypical careers, too. Your style—as well as your working and career choices—also depends on your own interests, what you excel at, and your own personal history. These characteristics are sometimes, but not always, type related.

TYPE FIVE

Many Fives choose specialized professions, using their strong informational and analytical skills to provide knowledge.

▶ **Technical Professions:** Many Fives excel in professions that allow for technical problem solving, such as computer science, coding, app and website development, technical support, technical writing, and mechanical skills.

▶ **Professor or Instructor:** Fives enjoy teaching their area of expertise and commonly find careers in science, mathematics, philosophy, business, and law.

- **Thought Leaders:** Some Fives are happily employed in think tanks or long-range policy positions, where they can use their independent thinking and long-range strategic analysis to solve large global problems.

- **Researchers:** Their strong curiosity leads many Fives to conduct or assist with many kinds of research. Fives thrive in science labs, fieldwork in psychology or archeology, theoretical explorations in mathematics or philosophy, or practical research that helps solve medical, business, or legal problems.

- **Engineers and Architects:** Both these positions require big-picture systematizing, original planning, and analytical skills, areas where many Fives excel.

- **Analyst:** A Five's patience and ability to synthesize large amounts of information makes them excellent at data, financial, or big-picture organizational analysis.

- **Public Information Provider:** More talkative Fives enjoy providing specialized information to the public as docents, tour guides, information booth attendants, and other similar roles.

Famous Fives in these occupations include Bill Gates and Marie Curie.

Fives also commonly choose to work in positions where they can be highly independent, often bringing originality to the role.

- **Management Consultant or Business Coach:** A Five's long-term approach makes them excellent at developing long-term strategies for businesses and employees, either as independent consultants or in an independent role in a company.

- **Writer:** Many Fives are excellent writers, and enjoy the independence of the role. It's common to see Fives write nonfiction, particularly around specialized knowledge or investigative research that they can condense for the public.

- ► **Artistic/Creative Professions:** Some Fives bring their strong originality and independent spirit to the arts, becoming film directors, novelists, artists, and musicians.

- ► **Startup Founder:** When Fives combine originality, independence, and a unique skillset, they're often very successful at founding startups, particularly in technical knowledge, or another area of special interest.

- ► **Remote Work:** Many Fives enjoy setting their own hours and taking on work they can do independently, such as grading, data entry, and proofreading.

Famous Fives in these occupations include Tim Burton and Joan Didion.

TYPE SIX

Sixes often end up in positions that have a defined structure and security, creating an environment where they can manage risk, or support others in doing so.

- ► **Finance:** Some Sixes are wonderful bankers, actuaries, or financial managers, providing a careful and structured approach that clients can trust.

- ► **Government:** Government positions at all levels allow Sixes to be the stewards of time-honored institutions that also provide a certain degree of job security.

- ► **Education:** As teachers, professors, and administrators, Sixes provide trustworthy care to the people or data they support, ensuring educational opportunities for future generations.

- ► **Science, Engineering, and Research:** Similar to academia, these fields come with established rules and standards to which Sixes can adhere while making their own contributions.

- ▶ **Ministry:** As ministers or clergy, Sixes protect religious traditions and provide caring pastoral support to the community at large.

- ▶ **Quality Assurance:** Sixes do a wonderful job as inspectors of health and safety facilities, or company auditors, carefully ensuring that health and quality standards are in place.

- ▶ **Project Management and Administrative Professionals:** Sixes make excellent project managers, as they can create structures that minimize risk and ensure all bases are covered by the team.

Famous Sixes in these occupations include George H. W. Bush and Princess Diana of Wales.

On the other hand, some Sixes thrive in high-pressure situations where they can get "down in the trenches" and provide high-volume action.

- ▶ **First Responders:** Sixes are often drawn to being firefighters, paramedics, and emergency room doctors and staff—people who can respond adeptly in times of crisis.

- ▶ **Mental Health and Addiction Support:** Some Sixes enjoy being active, hands-on, unshakeable support for people as psychologists, therapists, social workers, addiction counselors, and crisis hotline staff.

- ▶ **Police and Military:** Both of these positions combine participating in culturally defined and structured positions, while also offering the opportunity for risk, excitement, and saving lives.

- ▶ **Professional Advocates:** Sixes do a wonderful job defending those in need, whether they're directly involved in positions that support individuals (such as providing defense in a courtroom or other formal setting, or as healthcare advocates), or setting high-level policy.

- ▶ **Performers:** By combining toughness and vulnerability, many Sixes make excellent actors, comedians, and other performers—people who remind us of the full range of humanity in their delivery.

Famous Sixes in these occupations include David Letterman and Julia Roberts.

TYPE SEVEN

Sevens are often drawn to positions that allow for them to have maximum flexibility, spontaneity, and ability to generate endless possibilities on the job.

- ▶ **Directors:** It's particularly common to see Sevens directing ventures with a sense of fun, such as media agencies, retreat centers, or summer camps. Sevens in charge come up with numerous great ideas and have staff to execute them.

- ▶ **Entrepreneurs:** Many Sevens have the ability to generate endless ideas, and enjoy taking the kind of risks that starting a business requires. It's not uncommon to see Sevens as "serial entrepreneurs"—people who found one company or startup, make it successful, then move on to the next venture.

- ▶ **Generalist Professionals:** The gift of breadth and the ability to accomplish many things at once mean we see many Sevens in roles where they wear many hats, such as internal and emergency medicine, multilinguists, and managerial roles in business.

- ▶ **Marketing and Sales:** In both of these roles, Sevens can use their strengths for generating ideas and entertaining others to make sales, as well as to multitask and have variety in their workday.

- ▶ **Communication and Media:** Many Sevens enjoy the variety of interacting with others in fields such as social media, journalism, and other forms of mass communication.

- **Campaigners:** Particularly in new campaigns, Sevens get to create or execute ambitious plans from the ground up with freedom and spontaneity in their movements. These types of roles also allow them to be idealistic activists.

- **Travel-Related Professions:** As pilots, flight attendants, tour guides, travel writers, language teachers, and translators, Sevens get a sense of adventure and open-ended career potential.

Famous Sevens in these occupations include Richard Branson and Amelia Earhart.

Other Sevens are drawn specifically to roles where they can lift others up, using their ability to spread joy and happiness.

- **Helping Professions:** Certain Sevens are drawn to being therapists, counselors, and medical professionals, as they enjoy seeing the best in people and uplifting their spirits.

- **Event Planning and Executing:** Planning and fulfilling various event roles, such as catering or DJing, give Sevens the opportunity to create events that are fun and uplifting for others and themselves.

- **Work with Children:** Children are full of potential and fun to be with, so it's not surprising many Sevens enjoy working as child psychologists, pediatricians, teachers, special education professionals, childcare workers, and camp counselors.

- **Entertainers:** A sense of what they, and others, find amusing or thrilling makes Sevens engaging performers, musicians, comedians, and clowns—entertainers of any type.

- **Hospitality Industry:** Jobs like hotel employee, bartender, and restaurant server allow Sevens endless variety on the job, as well as opportunities to meet and entertain new people nightly.

- **Assistant:** A good attitude and the ability to do many things at once—and to make plans at the drop of a hat—make Sevens great personal assistants, stylists, gophers, or front-facing administrative professionals in offices.

Famous Sevens in these occupations include Robin Williams and Katy Perry.

TYPE EIGHT

Many Eights are drawn to occupations where they get to do impactful work from the top down, often in leadership positions.

- ▶ **Executive or CEO:** Whether in business, government, education, or nonprofits, the natural confidence and executive presence of Eights often leads them to high-level leadership positions.

- ▶ **Managers:** Eights often enjoy leading and being "on the ground" with people. They also have great energy and do well in managerial positions in business.

- ▶ **Business Founder or Entrepreneur:** The desire to call the shots and make immediate impact and change often leads Eights to start their own companies or move into entrepreneurial roles.

- ▶ **Political Organizers:** A desire to protect and support others means some Eights are drawn to work in policy or as campaign organizers—roles where they can create big changes.

- ▶ **Motivational Speaker:** Eights are wonderful at empowering and lifting people up. Motivational speeches allow them to deliver their message to large groups of people.

Famous Eights in these professions include Sheryl Sandberg and Dr. Martin Luther King Jr.

Other Eights like positions where they can feel immediacy and life through physical work or on-the-ground work with people.

- ▶ **Executive and Leadership Coaches:** Their innate confidence and natural ability to lead means Eights are excellent at coaching others to be better leaders or advance their rank at the office.

- ► **Property-Related Professions:** As general contractors, house flippers, property and commercial managers, handypeople, and landlords, Eights can work independently and on the ground in a way that creates a big impact and supports others.

- ► **Pilots and Truck Drivers:** Both these positions combine physical immediacy with big-impact, adventurous travel, and the ability to be one's own boss.

- ► **Military Officers:** In the military, Eights are given the opportunity to advance in leadership, protect and strengthen others, and find adventure.

- ► **Public Safety and Service:** As police officers, firefighters, paramedics, and other public safety officers, Eights have the opportunity to use their strengths to respond in crisis and help others in an immediate way.

- ► **Fitness Professionals:** Many Eights enjoy working with physicality and strength. It's not uncommon to see Eights excelling as athletes, athletic coaches, personal trainers, and gym teachers.

- ► **Security Guards:** Regardless of their physical stature, Eights know how to present a confident face. Many enjoy using their skills to protect banks, public areas, and entertainment venues.

Famous Eights in these professions include Napoleon Bonaparte and Serena Williams.

TYPE NINE

Often, Nines succeed in long-range, strategic work where they're able to create change in a slow, careful manner.

- ► **Leadership Positions:** Nines are so likeable that they often find themselves promoted to leadership positions in many industries: traditional business, government agencies, nonprofit organizations, et cetera. They excel in established institutions that need a consistent, steady, and slower-paced form of leadership.

- ▶ **Historians and Scientists:** Working as a historian, scientist, or in other academic and research-oriented fields allows Nines to create unified, holistic theories and observations—observations that require a deep understanding of how the past impacts the present. They're also patient teachers in their areas of strength.

- ▶ **Financial Positions:** Many Nines can be seen in various banking and other finance-related positions—positions that involve a conservative, long-range vantage point to make careful and important decisions. They can also make excellent business analysts.

- ▶ **Community Organizer:** An ability to bring others together, combined with patience and long-term strategizing skills, allows Nines to develop relationships and long-range planning that create change where it's needed.

- ▶ **Creative and Technical Professions:** Nines who are creatively or technically inclined have the patience and dedication needed to excel in art, music, web or graphic design, app development, writing, and other creative endeavors.

- ▶ **Outdoor Occupations:** Many Nines feel very connected to nature. They use their strengths in long-term planning to excel in agricultural fields, as park rangers, landscapers, and even construction workers.

Famous Nines in these occupations include Ronald Reagan and Whoopi Goldberg.

Other Nines enjoy working in occupations where they create a sense of harmony and peace for those around them.

- ▶ **Legal Mediator:** As mediators, Nines ensure that conflicts are resolved and harmony is maintained in difficult legal disputes. Nines can also be seen in other positions in the legal system.

- ▶ **Managers:** Nines are gentle and caring managers who tend to be popular with their employees. In managerial roles, they ensure conflict is minimized and harmony is maintained in the office.

- **Therapists:** It's particularly common to see Nines working as family therapists or couples' counselors—professions where they help create and maintain harmonious relationships. Nines also are patient, caring individual psychologists and therapists.

- **Early Childhood Professionals:** With seemingly endless patience, some Nines get great enjoyment out of helping young children grow. Nines can be drawn to working with young kids as educators, childcare workers, therapists, or pediatricians.

- **Animal Professionals:** Nines can feel an intuitive connection to animals, and may be drawn to working as veterinarians or animal trainers, or at zoos or in outdoor professions with nearby wildlife.

- **Athletic Professions:** Like Eights, Nines often feel connected to their bodies. They can be excellent athletes, often in individual sports. Their athletic knowledge and caring also lead them to be sports medicine doctors, physical therapists, and others who care for athletes.

Famous Nines in these occupations include Fred Rogers and Carl Jung.

THE ENNEAGRAM APPLIED

Work is just one of the practical arenas where people find the Enneagram useful. In learning about your type, you get a clearer sense of the personality-based skills you bring to your job and the ways you can best contribute. You also gain a better understanding of the people you work with, which is invaluable for resolving the high-stress situations that arise so often in collaborative environments. In the next chapter, we'll move from the office to the domestic sphere and look at another of the Enneagram's areas for practical application: relationship dynamics.

THE ENNEAGRAM IN RELATIONSHIPS

Humans are inherently social creatures. Our lives are deeply intertwined with the lives of others. We have longstanding, complex ties with our families. We value our friendships and collaborate with teams and colleagues in the office. We navigate networks in our workplaces and communities. Most of us seek out romantic relationships and partnerships. In our increasingly globalized world—a world where our online experiences intersect with in-person connections—managing our relationships has become more complex and important than ever. Relationships are important parts of our lives, and they come with their own sets of rewards and challenges.

When we talk with people about the Enneagram, the most common way they want to apply it is in their personal relationships. Often, they want to know what type their spouse or child is; they want to use the Enneagram as a springboard for understanding how to better connect with their loved ones. If they're single, they want to know what type of partner they should seek (more about that later). The good news is that the Enneagram can help with all of this.

In this chapter, we'll look at how each Enneagram type acts in relationships. We'll explore the gifts each type brings, and illuminate ways to connect with them. We'll dive into the world of dating and wade into the waters of family dynamics.

There's a lot to learn, so let's get started.

Overcoming Dating Fears

What do you do when you're hoping to find a romantic relationship, but aren't sure how? Julia's sister Mary provides a perfect example of this dilemma. A Type Six on the Enneagram, 30-year-old Mary works as a financial advisor in a different city from her family. She broke up with her longtime girlfriend a year ago and is looking to date again.

At her friends' suggestion, she's created a profile on one app, where she matched with an intriguing young therapist named Dasha. Suddenly, she has a message from Dasha waiting in her inbox, asking about some of the interests Mary listed on her profile and wondering if she would like to meet for coffee.

Mary worries that dating norms have changed since she last sought out romance. She fears that she'll make a faux pas, and wonders if she has what it takes to attract a good partner. What if Dasha meets her and decides Mary isn't as interesting as her profile? She can't help dreaming up worst-case scenarios. She wonders if she should decline the invitation. On her weekly Skype call with Julia, she asks for advice.

Julia isn't the first person Mary has asked for input. After a few leading inquiries, she finds out that Mary has asked several friends the same questions. "What should I do? What should I say? Should I pretend I didn't see the message?" Julia asks Mary if she would genuinely like to meet Dasha. "Of course!" Mary answers. "I'm just scared that I'll screw it up." Julia reminds Mary to listen to her inner voice—a voice that, at the moment, is encouraging her to get out there and meet people. If things don't work out with Dasha, there are many others she can connect with on the dating app.

Mary messages Dasha back, and they meet at her favorite coffee shop. In person, Dasha is more reserved than Mary, who finds herself doing most of the talking. At a few points, she stumbles over her words. Rather than laugh, Dasha smiles encouragingly. An apparent Nine on the Enneagram, Dasha has a gentle, reassuring manner that gradually puts Mary at ease. Mary finds herself drawing Dasha out in conversation. She is surprised to catch herself initiating plans for a second date, with eager anticipation and minimal worry about how it will go.

MEETING PEOPLE

No matter your type, you may be at a time in your life when you're seeking a new relationship. With networks of contacts and dating apps accessible at the flick of a finger, we have more tools at our disposal for finding romance than we've ever had before. Still, putting yourself out there can be nerve-racking. Here are some tips to guide each type in taking the plunge.

Type One: Ones tend to seek an ideal relationship, in line with their principles. Their "by the book" approach to dating means they often have a list of criteria they're looking for in a partner. Even so, the people Ones are drawn to rarely check all the boxes. Ones don't need to be perfect to attract the right mate: It may come as a surprise that dating can be fun. Rather than seeking a perfect match, Ones might try reaching out to people who seem intriguing. Stay open to the unexpected.

Type Two: To find love, Twos believe that they need to be loving and generous. Thus, Twos focus a lot on pleasing romantic prospects, adapting to others' needs and interests. They concentrate on getting to know, attracting, or showing appreciation for their dates rather than letting their own uniqueness shine through. Twos might try things the other way around: seek out people who share your passions; plan dates you'll personally find fun; and see what happens.

Type Three: Drawn to success and image, Threes value putting their best foot forward. They may focus on cultivating a particular look or persona to come across as desirable and admirable to their dates. However, too much image management may come at the expense of true connection. Focus less on impressing your dates and more on being genuine. Relax and let your guard down when you go out.

Type Four: Like Ones, Fours seek an ideal partner, but they're motivated by imagination rather than principles. They often fantasize about potential dates and may find themselves falling for a persona before getting to know the real person. Online dating or blind dates are particularly dangerous, so it's best to meet as early as feasible since the reality may not match the fantasy. Focus on genuinely connecting with your date. Be aware of your tendency to idealize.

Type Five: Passionate about their interests but awkward interpersonally, Fives tend to be reserved and take time to open up. It's helpful for Fives to build rapport by communicating for a while before meeting in person. Online dating can be a great fit. When you meet, try either a date around a mutual interest or a fun-filled activity where you let loose. Bringing delight into the equation will reduce nerves and discomfort. Bond around a subject of interest and conversation will flow easily.

Type Six: In search of a sure thing, Sixes seek a partner who's committed and dependable yet tend to be skeptical of finding one. They can be uncertain about the people they are seeing, asking others for their opinion. However, Sixes do best when listening to their internal response to dates instead of doubting themselves or consulting others. Rather than getting input from your "committee," go on a few dates where you focus on trusting your gut. Who and what feels right?

Type Seven: Sevens are drawn to options and dislike feeling pinned down. For some people of this type, dating seems like an exciting game, ripe with possibility. So many prospective dates, so little time! To get the most out of your dating experience, it's best to target your energy and explore purposefully. Focus on contacting just a few people at a time, and follow up if you'd like to pursue things further. If you're busy, take a break from looking into additional prospects.

Type Eight: Eights may enjoy the energy of dating, but when things get more personal or emotional, they often feel like fish out of water. Eights like being in charge on dates, but can sometimes seem intimidating or walled off, making it harder to establish relationships. Build connection by asking your dates about themselves. Show openness and caring, and allow your softer side to come out: it will be appreciated.

Type Nine: Nines go with the flow, making them laid-back dates and appealing to many. However, they find it challenging to take action toward their desires—or to even recognize their desires. Nines may want to date but hesitate to do so. If you're a Nine, assertiveness and momentum will go far. Try making the first move by contacting someone interesting. Then, make a concrete commitment to do something together.

The Types in Relationships

Let's take a look at what each type is looking for in a relationship, as well as their common relational strengths and pitfalls. Although this information is oriented toward romantic relationships, it can also be applied to your friendships, family connections, and professional relationships. Like the previous chapter on careers, these profiles look at common features and generalities within the Enneagram types. Specific details and behaviors can vary between individuals of the same type, depending on life experience, interpersonal dynamics, and each individual's level of psychological health. Healthier people are more resilient, understanding, and open in their relationships. Individuals at average levels of health and below are more likely to get into conflicts.

TYPE ONE: HIGH IDEALS

All the Enneagram types tend to look for partners who manifest the healthiest traits of their own type, and Ones are no exception. They tend to look for romantic relationships with people who conduct themselves with great integrity—people who are striving toward inherent goodness and improvement of themselves or the world around them. Ones are often drawn to partners with similar high-minded values, whether they're invested in political causes or a specific way of homemaking or raising children.

Often, Ones have a very specific idea of what they'd like in a partner, depending on what they personally view as a "good" or "right" match. The stereotype of creating a long list of criteria for an "ideal" partner comes from this type. This doesn't always have to be a written checklist. Often, it's something informal that's in the One's head.

ATTRIBUTES AND ATTITUDES

Healthy Ones are highly conscientious partners who aim to do the right thing in their relationships. They have a strong sense of morality and fairness, and consistently hold themselves to these standards with their partners. They are caring, compassionate, and appreciative of the efforts others make.

Average Ones can take out their frustrations on partners, being critical when they don't live up to their high ideals and standards in relationships. This can cause partners to feel hurt and unappreciated, particularly if the Type One partner doesn't always live up to the high standards that they preach themselves.

BUILDING A HEALTHY RELATIONSHIP

If you're partnered with a One, it's important to remember that criticisms and "you should" language directed toward you are often a sign of caring. Ones want their loved ones to be at their best at all times. Your partner is just trying to give you helpful suggestions. Usually, Ones aren't aware that their loving suggestions can be perceived as critical commentary.

Helping your One partner relax will ease their tension and rigidity. Many Ones can be physically tense: if your partner is one of them, offer to give them a massage, prepare a bath, or support them in finding another somatically relaxing activity. Find things you can do with your partner that they find fun. Give them permission to let loose a little bit by initiating and planning activities you both enjoy.

TYPE TWO: HEARTFELT BONDING

Twos are looking, first and foremost, for a heart-centered connection with their partners. Twos would like to build relationships with people who are genuinely loving—people who bring a sense of caring and appreciation to their relationships. Twos also appreciate partners who have a strong sense of empathy and are interested in developing relationships and connections.

Twos can also be drawn, intentionally or unintentionally, to relationships with people who they feel that they can help—they can "fix." For example, if a Two has a large network and enjoys developing relationships, they may be attracted to a partner who is shy or socially awkward. Or, if they enjoy caring for others through domestic tasks, they might partner with someone who has difficulty with or dislikes housework or outdoor fix-it work. This attraction of opposites helps a Two feel like they have something to offer in exchange for love.

ATTRIBUTES AND ATTITUDES

Healthy Twos tend to show a lot of warmth and appreciation for their partners, both verbally and through their actions. They tend to be intuitive about ensuring their needs are met. Twos will provide support in whatever genuine ways their partner needs help, and do so in a selfless and humble manner. They are sweet, emotionally connected, and inherently generous partners.

Average Twos can become manipulative in relationships. Sometimes, they can go overboard in their "helping," doing things their partners didn't need or ask for. They may expect excessive appreciation and help for their actions, becoming resentful and needy when their partner does not provide the kind of love they want.

BUILDING A HEALTHY RELATIONSHIP

When Twos start to help excessively, it's important to remember that what they're really seeking is emotional reassurance and love—whether or not they consciously realize it. Support your partner by appreciating them for the supportive help you need. When the behavior feels manipulative, determine what your partner's needs are and work to meet them.

Twos can be so focused on romantic relationships and caregiving that they neglect their own needs. Encourage your partner to explore their own interests. Genuinely compliment them for their skills unrelated to helping (for example, their intellectual prowess). Give them the opportunity to try new things by themselves, even if these things don't interest you. Gently nudge them toward self-care activities that interest them.

Busting Myths About Compatibility *"What type am I most compatible with?" If we had a quarter for every time we've heard that question, we could treat ourselves to dinner. Compatibility is complex. While relationships between any two types have predictable highs and lows (see the Resources section on page 161), people of the same type may be drawn to different personalities, depending on formative experience and personal preference. It's most important to find a partner who shares your values and goals. As Enneagram teacher Tom Condon suggests, look for "a healthy type and one who loves you!"*

TYPE THREE: THE REAL DEAL

Threes are drawn to partners who value authenticity. They appreciate partners who are motivated, goal-oriented, and committed to a life that reflects themselves. Threes appreciate partners who work hard, but also those who create a harmonious work/life balance and demonstrate effort and sincerity in making the relationship work.

Threes are often looking for an "ideal" person to be their partner. What "ideal" means can vary based on family and cultural expectations. For example, some Threes may want a partner who is a quiet, domestically oriented homemaker, while others may prefer someone in a high-powered career who "does it all." Average Threes may also seek out relationships that look good externally: a partner their family approves of, someone who looks good for the Three's professional image, or even a relationship that appears "edgy."

ATTRIBUTES AND ATTITUDES

Healthy Threes bring their best selves to relationships, offering value to their partners by doing whatever it is they do best. They remain inspired to work on themselves and their relationships, often motivating their partner to do the same. They're proud of what their partner brings. They know how to compliment their partners and make them feel valued.

Average Threes can become slippery in relationships. They can seem like they're trying to "sell" themselves to a partner, leaving the partner to wonder who their loved one really is. They also tend to be workaholics, neglecting their relationships at the expense of achieving their own success.

BUILDING A HEALTHY RELATIONSHIP

Remember that when your Three partner is demanding attention for themselves, what they really seek is validation and approval. Appreciate your Three partner when they do something valuable, whether it's helping out around the house or giving a successful presentation at work. Create a safe space where they can express uncertainty and doubt with you. Invite them to open up and connect with you.

Encourage your Three partner to unplug from time to time. Plan a relaxing day for them to spend with you, or suggest they participate in practices to connect with themselves. Eschewing lavish or fast-paced dates for quieter activities can help Threes stay aligned with their hearts, making them deeply committed and caring romantic partners.

TYPE FOUR: DIVING DEEP

Fours appreciate romantic partners who bring emotional depth to their relationships. They look for relationships where heartfelt honesty is shared between both partners, and value partners who are interested in pursuing their own personal growth. Fours are also looking for partners who can mirror them—partners who can help them feel seen and acknowledged in the relationship.

Fours are prone to fantasizing, and a common fantasy is that of a perfect partner who will save them. Like the Three, the ideal partner will vary from Four to Four. A common theme among Fours is that their partner will be perfect and ultimately complete them. When entering relationships, Fours are prone to idealizing their new partners in this way.

ATTRIBUTES AND ATTITUDES

Healthy Fours are deeply devoted partners who inspire rich creativity and growth in the relationship. They encourage their partners to seek and find themselves. They allow for vulnerable and honest sharing from their partners and fundamentally understand the emotional ups and downs of relationships.

Average Fours can become frustrated with their partners because they don't live up to the ideal lover they envisioned. As a result, Fours can become critical of their partners. They can also be emotionally volatile and hard to pin down, potentially leaving their partners confused and upset.

BUILDING A HEALTHY RELATIONSHIP

Beneath the emotional volatility Fours sometimes show, they're ultimately looking to be seen and validated by their partners. Approaching a Four who is acting moody with your own display of emotional volatility will just amp them up more. Instead, do your best to remain steadfast, confident, and grounded through challenges. Providing your Four partner with calm, soothing validation will help them calm down and be able to see themselves in a way that's less self-critical.

Physically grounding or soothing activities will help bring your Four partner out of their fantasies and down to earth, more engaged in and appreciative of the immediate relationship they have with you. You can also encourage your Four partner to express their emotions through a creative project of their choice, giving them a supportive outlet for their feelings.

TYPE FIVE: MEETING OF MINDS

Fives are attracted to partners who bring intellectual depth and clarity to the relationship. They enjoy a natural exchange of ideas in relationships, often gravitating toward those where their partner shares their same special interests—or that at least allow them an opportunity to pursue their own interests.

Commonly, Fives look for relationships where they can have a lot of time and space to themselves. Often Fives feel easily overwhelmed by the demands of life. Space in relationships helps them feel less overwhelmed by their partner. They can also have a lack of interest in handling the practical and social aspects of life, and look for partners who are able to help them in these areas.

ATTRIBUTES AND ATTITUDES

Healthy Fives are endlessly curious, bringing all kinds of interesting information and innovative ideas to their partners. They are supportive, share openly about themselves, and can laugh with at the absurdities of life. They are patient with their partners and take a long-range view of the relationship.

Average Fives can be distant and unavailable to their partners, getting too distracted by their minds and interests to participate in family or emotional life. Their partners can feel like they need to get these needs met elsewhere. Average Fives can also be cynical, bringing argumentativeness and a general negative attitude about people into their romantic partnership.

BUILDING A HEALTHY RELATIONSHIP

When Fives become emotionally unavailable, it's usually because they're overwhelmed, rather than trying to be intentionally hurtful. When Fives close up, patience and support is key, as is creating an environment that makes them feel emotionally safe about opening up in the relationship. Ask them to open up one-on-one, in an intimate setting, rather than, say, in a loud restaurant with a group of friends.

One way to get Fives to open up and trust you is to ask them about their favorite intellectual interests. From there, conversations can grow more intimate and personal. Fives also benefit from physical activities—activities that allow them to be grounded and connect with their bodies. Participate in these activities with your partner, or encourage your partner to do them independently. Fives who are grounded in this way become more confident and open in their romantic relationships.

TYPE SIX: THROUGH THICK AND THIN

Sixes look for partners who bring a sense of deep, unshakeable support and direction into the relationship. All types desire partners who are committed to them, but Sixes are particularly interested in knowing their relationship will be with them through thick and thin. Sixes appreciate partners who are trustworthy, hardworking, and steadfast.

Sixes can have a sense of uncertainty and anxiety about their relationships, even if they've been married for decades. The nervousness that their partner isn't supporting them and isn't committed enough to the relationship always exists. Sixes look for partners who are unwavering, even as the Six questions their partner's commitment to them.

ATTRIBUTES AND ATTITUDES

Healthy Sixes bring a deep sense of guidance, grounded love, and commitment into relationships. They are able to lead the relationship, and their romantic partner, in directions that best support them. They are team-oriented people, and typically work for what is best for the common good of the relationship.

Average Sixes can be erratic partners, constantly worried about worst-case scenarios and what might go wrong in a relationship. Fear and paranoia may cause them to make unfounded accusations of disloyalty toward their partners, causing their partners, ironically, to develop mistrust of the Six.

BUILDING A HEALTHY RELATIONSHIP

The anxiety and doubt Sixes can feel about their relationship comes from their own "swinging pendulum" and racing thoughts—which then get projected onto their partner. As the partner to a Six, remember not to take this personally. The best thing you can do for your partner is to stay confident, solid, and unwavering in the face of their uncertainty and doubt.

Sixes become more solid in relationships through their own grounding, through connecting with their bodies and "checking in" with logic and reason. Resist the urge to get argumentative. Doing so will only make your partner more anxious. Instead, counter their fears with calmness and clear logic. Encourage your partner to use their nervous energy to get physically active, and to focus and accomplish key tasks.

TYPE SEVEN: ADVENTURE TOGETHER

Sevens look for relationships that bring a sense of fun and joy to their lives. Sevens can see life as a great adventure. As a result, they often look for romantic partners who will live out adventures with them, bringing life to something as routine as a trip to a grocery store. Sevens value upbeat, positive people who can also be there with them in difficult times.

With desire for novelty and variety, Sevens are stereotyped as having a difficult time committing to monogamous relationships. In fact, some Sevens may prefer casual dating or open relationships to monogamy. Other Sevens, however, are very committed to one partner. Instead, they look for novelty within their relationship or in other areas of their life.

ATTRIBUTES AND ATTITUDES

Healthy Sevens are delightful partners who create boundless opportunities in their lives. They can lift the spirits of their partner, and are able to be enthusiastic about every aspect of their relationship and life together. Partners of healthy Sevens will rarely be bored by their relationships.

Average Sevens can be highly distractible, sometimes over-committing and neglecting their partners as a result. They can get frustrated quickly and have a difficult time listening to any negativity from their partners, or admitting to negative feelings within themselves.

BUILDING A HEALTHY RELATIONSHIP

It can be difficult for Sevens to be satisfied by what's in front of them, leading to a "grass is greener" mentality. When Sevens appear bored, frustrated, or fickle in relationships, it's the result of this mindset, not because their partner has limited their options or held them back.

Sevens become happier and more stable partners when they take the time to go inward and connect with themselves, particularly their feelings and emotions. Don't try to stop your partner's desire to do many things at once. Instead, encourage them to cultivate a regular gratitude practice, or something similar that they enjoy. If they stick to this, Sevens will calm down and ground, becoming deeply appreciative of their feelings and their romantic relationships.

TYPE EIGHT: MOVING AND SHAKING

Eights look for romantic partners who can live fully and be real with them. Natural leaders, Eights often like to feel like they're in charge in relationships. However, they also appreciate partners who value and support their emotional needs.

Eights like to support people who they see as being "weaker" than themselves and can be drawn to partners whom they feel they can protect. They desire romantic relationships where they feel strong, confident, and in control. As movers and shakers, they also like it when their partner can keep up with their active, fast-paced lives.

ATTRIBUTES AND ATTITUDES

Healthy Eights are confident and inspiring partners, grounded and solid in their relationships and lives. They work hard to provide unshakeable support for their partners, whether financial, physical, or whatever else is needed. They are openhearted souls, and gentle under their tough exteriors.

Average Eights can become aggressive and confrontational in relationships, asserting themselves to make sure they get their way in relationships. Their bravado, tough talking, and self-confidence can be intimidating or even scary for their romantic partners.

BUILDING A HEALTHY RELATIONSHIP

Eights become intimidating and confrontational in relationships because they secretly fear not being strong or tough enough—that, in turn, people will reject them. Eights respect people who are confident themselves, and respond positively to a partner who can appear unflinching during a conflict. An Eight who respects their partner will be more egalitarian in how they view their relationship.

It also helps to be soft and tenderhearted with your Eight partner, as this can break down their defenses. Be gentle and reassuring to the Eight in your life. Encourage them to do activities that really make them feel nurtured. You can also support them in developing regularity and routine in their lives—both of which help regulate their anger and keep them on a more even keel, emotionally.

TYPE NINE: PEACE AND UNITY

Nines seek out partners with whom they feel they can have peaceful, harmonious relationships. Most Nines desire unified and stable partnerships, where they can feel calm, reassured, and in balance. Often, they like partners who take the lead in relationships, whose lives they can join and become a part of. Some Nines are very physically active and like partners who can do physical activities with them.

It's not uncommon to see Nines choose partners who they can feel merged with, sharing values and life desires. Although all Enneagram types desire this, in Nines this can be more extreme. They fear any disagreement could lead to a lack of harmony in the relationship.

ATTRIBUTES AND ATTITUDES

Healthy Nines are calm, gentle, and supportive partners. They have positive outlooks. They know how to smooth over difficult situations and keep the peace. They can be stabilizing for partners who are naturally more emotionally reactive or pessimistic. Many of them bring creativity and a connectedness to nature into their relationships.

Average Nines can be overly conflict-avoidant in romantic relationships. Sometimes, they may not even want to admit that there's a conflict in the first place. At times, Nines will say they agree with their partners, while dragging their feet or lashing out in anger, causing their partners to get irritated and angry with them.

BUILDING A HEALTHY RELATIONSHIP

Nines can be self-effacing in relationships, engaging in passive-aggressive behavior because they genuinely want happy partners and harmonious relationships. Nines can also feel unimportant and unseen. In this case, give your partner compliments and recognition, assuring them that you want to hear their voice and opinions as much as needed.

Many Nines love physical activity. It can help ground them and give them the opportunity to express their own needs. Encourage your partner to participate in slow-paced, intentional movement, such as karate, or they may check out and become disengaged in their activity. Many Nines also find spending time outdoors grounding and soothing. Spend time in nature with your partner, and support them confidently in their own personal endeavors.

RESOLVING RELATIONSHIP CONFLICTS

Part of the beauty of relationships is that each participant brings a different perspective. This, of course, also means that our perspectives sometimes clash. Think of the last time a conflict arose in an important relationship for you: Did one person want to use logic, while the other focused on emotions? Maybe one of you urged the other to look on the bright side.

When a clash of perspectives gets out of control, it can leave scars in our relationships. When approached with attention and empathy, conflicts become opportunities for understanding each other and deepening our bonds. The Enneagram's conflict resolution styles are useful tools for keeping relationship conflicts positive and solution-focused. As you review the styles below, consider which approaches you and your loved ones lead with.

- ▶ **The Competency Types** (One, Three, and Five) bring an analytical approach to conflict. Their style might be stated succinctly as, "Let's act like adults here and solve things logically." Their rational solution strategy maintains civility at the risk of seeming overly cool. People with other styles may find themselves frustrated by a Competency-based loved one's detachment.

- ▶ **The Emotional Realness Types** (Four, Six, and Eight) seek to bring emotional truths into the open. This style is helpful for unearthing the underlying dynamics of conflicts, but risks creating a cycle of reactivity. People with other styles may be annoyed by a loved one's Emotional Realness focus on problems over solutions.

- ▶ **The Positive Outlook Types** (Two, Seven, and Nine) look at the larger context of a problem, focusing on existing positives and seeking the best possible outcome. While this style raises morale, it may also overlook or neglect a conflict's knotty aspects. People with other styles may be irritated when a loved one sweeps the problem under the rug.

When used individually, each conflict resolution style is wonderful for addressing one aspect of a problem, but tends to neglect other important elements. In order to effectively resolve conflict, it's best to use the three styles together. If you and your loved one have different styles, rather than clashing over your divergent approaches, recognize that they bring different valuable tools to the table. When things get tough between you, make a conscious effort to use the third style to address your collective blind spot. If you share a style, try consciously bringing in the other two perspectives.

You can approximate the approaches of all three styles by following a three-step conflict resolution process. First, tap into the strengths of the Emotional Realness style by identifying underlying tensions and naming the roots of the conflict. Next, use the Competency style's focus on logical problem solving to brainstorm potential solutions. Finally, as the Positive Outlook Types do, look at the larger context, e.g., asking yourself, "Will this matter in five years?" Seek a way to address the conflict that will yield positive results for all parties.

Communication Styles

Communication is one of the most important skills for building and sustaining interpersonal relationships. Each type has its own way of communicating and trying to get its needs met. Sometimes, conflicts can arise when people with different Enneagram types misunderstand each other and jump to conclusions—often assuming that a person with a different type communicates similarly to how they do!

By learning how each style communicates, you'll become more understanding and better able to resolve disagreements and breakdowns in communication. Here's a breakdown of each type's communication style.

Ones communicate directly and precisely. Their communication can include a lot of "shoulds," and their voices can display tension and frustration. A challenge for Ones is to avoid being too preachy in conversations and displaying irritation with others who are not "right."

Ones should aim to speak in a way that is relaxed and accepting toward others. To communicate with Ones, speak to the effort you are making, and ground your conversation in common values.

Twos often communicate in a way that is warm and enticing. They have a tendency to focus on others, with flattery and gushy expressions. A challenge for Twos is to avoid "leaning in" too much to other people, making them uncomfortable. Twos should aim to communicate with others in a way that displays compassion through thoughtful, targeted directives and emotional restraint. To communicate with Twos, show appreciation and be attentive to your personal connection.

Threes communicate in a way that is competent, efficient, and smooth. They can be chameleonic and highly adaptable to their audience. A challenge for Threes is to avoid making conversations into "sales pitches" that draw attention to themselves. Threes should aim to communicate in a tone that is genuine, caring, and attuned to the emotional needs of other people. When communicating with Threes, take a direct, goal-oriented approach. Tactful honesty is appreciated.

Fours typically communicate in a way that is personal and emotionally honest. Fours can speak at length about feelings, to get emotional responses from others. A challenge for Fours is to avoid speaking in a way that is dramatic but also erratic and ungrounded. Fours should aim to communicate in a way that is physically embodied and uses rationality to back up feelings. When communicating with Fours, acknowledge their emotions and be up front about your own. Show that you respect them as individuals.

Fives communicate in a way that tends to be specific and cerebral, focused on thoughts and ideas. A challenge for Fives is to avoid speaking in a way that is emotionally dry and detached. It's helpful for Fives to cultivate interest and conversational attention to others' thoughts and feelings. Fives should aim to meet other people from a place of heartfelt care and engagement in their stories. To communicate with Fives, engage them intellectually and show an interest in their ideas. If you're curious, you may learn a lot.

Sixes are typically warm and engaged. Sixes often speak nervously and are self-effacing. A challenge for Sixes is to avoid displaying anxiety about where they stand with others by testing and challenging people in conversations. Sixes should aim to speak in a way that is grounded and displays confidence in what they are saying. To communicate with Sixes, be steady in your decisions and reassuring toward them. Show that you are loyal and reliable.

Sevens typically communicate fast and enthusiastically. Sevens are upbeat and often spin stories. A challenge for Sevens is to avoid speaking in a way that sounds demanding, impatient, and focused on their immediate needs at the expense of the other person. They should aim to speak in a way that is calm, focused, and accepting of others. When communicating with Sevens, echo their enthusiasm and share your own, while being pragmatic about needs and goals.

Eights communicate in a way that is filled with energy. Eights tend to be straightforward and blunt; others will know where they stand with them. A challenge for Eights is to avoid being overly callous and argumentative with others. They should aim to communicate in a way that is heartfelt and compassionate toward others' feelings and needs. When communicating with Eights, be direct and match their energy level. Don't be afraid to get into a good debate.

Nines communicate gently and reflectively. They can have a tendency to ramble, telling long stories or sagas before getting to the point. A challenge for Nines is to avoid being too passive and going along with others in conversations. Nines should aim to speak in a way that is confident and directly expresses themselves. To communicate with Nines, be accepting and patient in your approach. Allow them space to get in touch with and express their opinions.

Family Relationships and Roles

Navigating our family dynamics can sometimes be even more complex than finding and maintaining a romantic relationship. Generally, we choose our spouse or romantic partner, but not our parents, siblings, children, or extended family members. At times, we have wonderful organic compatibility with our family of origin. But, in other cases, our loved ones are quite different from the people we choose to befriend or date. Most of us will change friends or romantic relationships at some point in our life, but our families typically stay with us for life. Learning how to navigate these relationships is especially important.

All families are unique, but each Enneagram type tends to play a particular role in their individual family dynamic. Understanding the role you usually fall into around your family can shed light on new options and alternative ways of interacting with them.

Type One: Ones fill the role of the family perfectionist, fulfilling parents' expectations to the letter or instilling values and standards in their children.

Type Two: Twos fall into the role of family helper, pleasing their parents or diligently looking after their children's needs.

Type Three: Threes fulfill the role of family star, embodying their parents' values and dreams or encouraging their kids to succeed.

Type Four: Fours shed light on the family's problems, encouraging their loved ones to address difficult familial shadows.

Type Five: Fives prefer to have some space from family dynamics, and seek the role of family expert in areas of interest.

Type Six: Sixes move between building family unity and rebelling against the family unit. They're often rebellious children and protective parents.

Type Seven: Sevens fill the role of family cheerleader, bringing smiles to family members and seeking to minimize pain.

Type Eight: Eights become family protectors, exerting power as children or parents and taking on responsibility for loved ones.

Type Nine: Nines act as family peacemakers, mediating conflicts between parents or children and refusing to take sides.

STRENGTHENING
CONNECTIONS

Think of the relationships that are important to you. How does your Enneagram type impact the way you interact with these key people? What gifts does it bring to your relationships? What habits do you have that make it challenging for you to connect?

Consider the Enneagram types of others who are important in your life. How are they seeing the world differently from you? What do they most want out of their relationship with you? What's one thing you can do for each important person this week to show them that you get them and appreciate the connection you share? Commit to taking one small action for each person you care about.

NAVIGATING FAMILY DYNAMICS

In order to see how the Enneagram can help improve family dynamics, let's return to Julia as she spends time with her immediate family during the holiday season.

Julia is excited for the winter holidays because her sister, Mary, is visiting from out of town. Her boyfriend, Miguel, is going to celebrate with her family, too, rather than with his parents as he usually does. Julia and Miguel pick Mary up at the airport, and Julia immediately launches into plans of all the fun activities they'll do together: baking, skiing, playing long rounds of family card games. . .

Her enthusiasm dims when her parents and Mary greet each other. Their mother, Evelyn, is a Type Eight, and orders Mary to put her things away while brusquely telling her the plans for the day. Always the family rebel, Mary resists, refusing some activities and suggesting alternatives to others. "I'm your mother," Evelyn insists. "You do what the family wants, and we'll have a good holiday together!" "No," Mary insists, beginning to regret her decision to stay at her parents' house.

"I need to settle in first. And I see no reason the rest of us have to watch that same holiday special for the 10 millionth time when no one but you even likes it!" Her father, Steve, an Enneagram Five, hangs back from the argument as usual. As the two women's voices grow heated, he retreats into the living room.

Miguel's first holiday with Julia's entire immediate family proves challenging. True to his type as a Two, he tries to be useful by mediating between Evelyn and Mary. Both resist what they see as a pushy outside influence. Julia suggests a different set of holiday activities to the family and is able to get everyone engaged. However, by the fifth energetic game, Steve is overwhelmed and heads to bed early. Mary is disappointed that her father would rather go off by himself than spend time with her when she has come to visit from far away. Does he not care about her enough?

Family dynamics are tricky to navigate because they develop over the course of years and involve deep emotional investment from all parties. Often, different family members want different things, but without knowing each other's motivations, everyone imagines their family members are just "being obnoxious." An Enneagram intervention can help clarify and address the underlying dynamics.

Julia introduces the Enneagram types to her feuding family, and they laugh in recognition. Evelyn wants to be in charge. Steve wants space and hates being overwhelmed. Mary wants reassurance and autonomy. Julia wants things to be fun, and Miguel wants to establish connections with his partner's family. How can everyone get what they want?

Steve's analytical mind comes up with a solution. Maybe Evelyn can suggest activities with the understanding that the others will choose which ones they want to participate in. He reassures Mary and Julia that he loves seeing them, but also doesn't want to do energy-draining activities the whole time they're there, a stance they can understand. Evelyn suggests that Steve lead an activity he prefers, and he entertains everyone with tales of holiday history. Miguel finds a new way of connecting and being helpful by pitching in with kitchen duties rather than trying to mend relationships. With a clearer understanding of each other, Julia's family members are free to divide and participate in activities as they please. Rather than pushing each other, they respect each other's boundaries, leading to a more fun and pleasant time for all.

Your family, like Julia's, is probably full of diverse personalities with very different needs. The Enneagram can be useful for understanding where everyone is coming from and ensuring these needs get met. Look beyond the surface and seek compromises that satisfy different people's core motivations. You might find that your family dynamic changes for the better.

In the next chapter, we'll look beyond family and work to ways the Enneagram can help you grow as a person.

GROWTH
AND CHANGE

On this Enneagram journey, we've talked about different aspects of the system and discovered ways you can apply them to improve your career and relationships. Along with using your Enneagram knowledge in practical ways, you may also be interested in applying it on a deeper level. There are many ways you can use the Enneagram to notice and change unhelpful habits, build resilience, and craft a more balanced, happier life for yourself. This chapter will explore a few starting points for creating a solid foundation of ongoing personal growth.

The Enneagram and Growth

Some people new to the Enneagram mistakenly believe that once they discover their type, they have exhausted the system's usefulness. While it can be tempting to feel like we're "finished" after learning our type, there's more to it than that. Besides, if we learn our own personality type without using that knowledge to work on ourselves, we won't grow. By working on ourselves, we're able to find freedom from our ingrained habits and patterns.

The Enneagram is a uniquely useful tool for growth and change because it delves deeply into our core motivations. While other well-known personality typologies do an excellent job measuring and explaining human behaviors and personality traits, the Enneagram describes us at a deeper level. It explains *why* we act in certain ways. Seeing what drives our behavior allows us to examine our deeply held beliefs, attitudes, and choices, offering a level of insight that's hard to reach without this kind of road map.

The Enneagram also brings amazing breadth and depth to personal development. When used correctly, as a dynamic system for change rather than as a means of stereotyping and judging, it describes the full range of our behaviors. Along with the insights we get from learning our primary Enneagram type, we gain additional wisdom about ourselves when we learn about our connections to other types through wings, Stress Points, and Security Points. When we consider the healthy, average, and unhealthy sides of our type, or look at these in more detail using Riso and Hudson's Nine Levels of Development (see *Personality Types* and *Understanding the Enneagram* for further reading), we have a map that describes ourselves from our absolute best to very worst days.

Regardless of cultural background and life experiences, the core psychological structure of our Enneagram type remains consistent. This makes the Enneagram a growth tool that works for all demographics and can facilitate understanding between them. You can be any race, gender, socioeconomic status, and religion, and still benefit from the Enneagram. All that's needed is a desire to grow.

HOW NOT TO USE
THE ENNEAGRAM

"I'm a Seven, so I can never finish what I start!"

"Of course you're angry at me. You're an Eight!"

We've heard sentences like these in the Enneagram world, and they tend to make us cringe. While the Enneagram types are incredible tools for understanding human behavior, it's not unusual for people to grab ahold of them as ways of excusing that behavior rather than as tools for change. If you notice yourself using your knowledge of the Enneagram types to stereotype or write off actions—yours or someone else's—take a second look. Having a certain type doesn't mean that your behavior is set in stone. Think about the unhealthy, average, and healthy ranges in each type: They're all part of that type's potential. How can you look beyond the annoying habits sometimes found at the types' average levels toward the possibility of dynamism and growth?

The Enneagram is a great tool for facilitating change. What's just as important is the fact that the self-awareness Enneagram work brings is a doorway to self-acceptance. Many people describe feeling a sense of relief when they find their Enneagram type. Most of us feel a great sense of reassurance when we finally gain an explanation for why we keep getting caught in the same traps. Through the Enneagram, not only do we learn that our personality's challenges aren't our fault, we also get glimpses of our greatest possibilities and gifts. We stop blaming ourselves for our shortcomings and see the beauty in our true selves. We begin to love ourselves for exactly who we are.

THE BENEFITS OF
SELF-AWARENESS

The road to self-realization is not always obstacle free. When we work on ourselves, we see things about ourselves that we didn't see before. While these things can be positive and heartwarming, sometimes we learn things about ourselves that we don't like. Other times, we uncover past hurt and sorrow. The journey is unpredictable.

Luckily, the rewards for doing this work are immense. Below are five benefits you will get from working on yourself and developing self-awareness.

1. **Your coping skills will improve.** Life will always throw challenges at you. When you lack self-awareness, you may address obstacles from a place of reactivity, and it becomes much harder to cope. With awareness, you can handle these difficulties from a place of grace and acceptance, and it becomes easier to remain positive and relaxed, and to make empowering choices.

2. **You will heal yourself.** When pain remains buried and unaddressed, hurt lingers on in your body, making you more likely to react to the present from the place of your past pain. Working through your challenges makes it easier to act consciously and frees you from the burdens you carry. People tend to feel much better each time an issue gets resolved.

3. **Your internal sense of balance will increase.** Sometimes, you may feel as if you are on an emotional tightrope. Each emotion and reaction has the potential to hit you like a strong gust of wind, leaving you struggling to cling to the delicate balance you've created. Self-awareness gives you strength, and acceptance makes you even stronger. You can maintain your balance and weather internal storms.

4. **Your relationships will get better.** You can make it easy for others to enjoy your company when you relate to them from a place of awareness. When you react to others from a place of unconsciousness, you have more conflicts, and greater hurt may arise in relationships. With self-awareness, you develop compassion for others' pain. It is easier to connect with others from a place of kindness.

5. **You will develop presence and mindfulness.** Being present allows people to live in the here and now. When we are focused on only the current moment, we don't need to feel hurt by the wounds from the past or fear the unknown in the future. We find acceptance and joy in everything. We simply are. In presence, we see others and ourselves fully and compassionately.

Living with Accountability

We are all works in progress. Some areas of life are easy for us, while other domains present obstacles. We have many traits and habits that we're conscious of, and others that are hard for us to see. The Enneagram empowers us to get more in touch with our internal states, desires, and needs. If you're looking to use the Enneagram to create positive change in your life, one of the keys to doing this is knowing yourself and becoming accountable to yourself.

As you learn about your type, look out for desires and motivations that you've been discounting in yourself. For example, are you a people person working in a field with little interpersonal interaction? Do you want more power or visibility, but hold yourself back from pursuing these things in a satisfying way? Due to various forms of cultural conditioning, many of us write off important parts of ourselves because they're "inappropriate," "undesirable," "too much" this, or "not enough" of that. When we do this, we deny the gifts that we could bring into the world. We can only bring balance into our lives if we accept the people we are in the first place, and make choices that fit our personality's needs. Listen to your type's desire for integrity, clarity, harmony, or whatever is at the core, and look for healthy ways to let it guide you.

Just as we deny some of our gifts, we also tend to overlook our own unhelpful habits. Take an honest look at the descriptions of your type's average and unhealthy sides. Which tendencies do you see in yourself? Take a day to observe your Enneagram patterns at work. Notice whenever you're acting out your type's habits in a way that's detrimental. Riso and Hudson call this "catching yourself in the act." Practice this type of awareness every day. With time, your ability to observe yourself will grow. You'll develop an ability that Helen Palmer calls the "inner observer"—that quiet place inside yourself, distinct from your reactions, that watches your mind without participating in its chatter. As you think and act, the inner observer takes everything in. It brings critical distance and the ability to pause, rethink, and change your usual way of doing things. The more you flex the muscles of the inner observer, the more control you will have over your habits and the more conscious choices you will make.

Living in harmony with your type's motivations and developing an inner observer are ways of being accountable to yourself. However, it's challenging to do these things alone. The path to personal growth gets much easier when you enlist some traveling companions. It's helpful to have a partner, family member, or friend (or more than one) to do Enneagram work with. Together, you can candidly talk type, call each other out when needed, and support each other's efforts to live with accountability. It's even more supportive to find a community of people committed to personal growth. Some people find this in religious or spiritual groups, or in groups focused on a specific practice. These bring support, community, alternative perspectives, and a place to focus on yourself. Seek out a group that meets regularly—one you can be open with and whose principles you find supportive. Seeking a mix of personal connections and a wider group context oriented to growth brings guidance and support as you connect with yourself and move forward.

RECOGNIZING AND CHANGING BAD HABITS

Let's get back to the inner observer for a minute. It's a tricky thing to develop because we're used to acting out our habits rather than noticing them. All of us live our daily lives as creatures of our habits, from our morning coffee, to our work schedules, all the way down to our preferred bedtime. Our habits are external, what we do in our daily lives, and internal, as driven by our personalities. Our egos dictate our habitual inner self-talk, driven by our personality type and personal life experiences. This self-talk is largely unconscious, and when we react to this talk instead of cultivating an awareness of the immediate world around us, it's harder to make the right choices to support our own lives.

As you begin paying attention to these daily habits, the things you do when you aren't making deliberate choices, you'll hear self-talk in the back of your mind. As with your habits, this dialogue has probably been following you around all your life without you paying much attention to it. It sounds like the voice of "the way things are." Listen to it without judgment, bringing gentleness and curiosity. While your own personal dialogue will be unique, here are some common themes that appear in the unconscious talk of each type:

Type One: Ones have strong inner critics, and their internal voice can sound particularly parental. There's a strong sense of responsibility, and of things that they "must" do in order to be a good person. Ones are driven to act in the world largely based on this heavy internal dialogue of inner criticism.

Type Two: The Two inner voice often speaks about other people the Two is in relationship with. Twos will focus on the "other"—what that person needs, and how to provide support. This encourages Twos to provide acts of services, in the hope that true love will come from their efforts.

Type Three: Threes unconsciously are always looking for ways they can be the best at whatever they're doing. They hear their family's voice: specifically, what they perceived their family wanted them to do to be successful. This causes them to go out and achieve in ways they believe will make them valuable.

Type Four: After taking action or having intimate conversations, Fours will instantly check in with how they're doing emotionally. The current feelings get absorbed into the Four's internal self-image. Fours will then react based on their most current self-perception, which frequently involves negative comparisons or idealization.

Type Five: A Five's inner dialogue will always be looking for ways they can learn or know more about a subject or situation, usually in great depth. By continuing to dig deeper and deeper for knowledge, Fives hope that they will finally feel like they know enough to confidently take action in the world.

Type Six: Russ Hudson describes the Six inner voice as being like a pendulum: anxiously swinging from place to place, looking for a true source of safety, security, and guidance. Their anxiety-producing inner dialogue causes them to look outside of themselves for a stable, reassuring place of security.

Type Seven: A Seven's self-talk is often extremely positive, seeking out the next fun, exciting source of stimulation. A Seven's thoughts commonly move rapidly, looking for satisfaction and fulfillment from a wide variety of sources. They react by going out into the world and looking for new ways to find happiness.

Type Eight: The habitual dialogue of Eights gets bigger and bigger: looking to sound bolder, stronger, and more confident with each thought. By creating dialogue that's full of confidence and bluster, Eights are trying to drown out the voices of sensitivity and doubt, and the fear they aren't strong enough.

Type Nine: Nines talk to themselves in a way that's relatively positive ("I'm okay, you're okay"), but can also feel secretly resigned to the way things are. They'll imagine what is nice in their present lives. This kind of talk keeps them in a bubble of internal comfort, stopping them from taking possibly earth-rattling risks.

The first step to changing your inner habits is just being aware of what they are. Through awareness, you can make a conscious effort to introduce different self-talk that slowly changes your internalized beliefs. This kind of change takes time: you've been doing your type's patterns for years, after all, and research shows it typically takes a couple of months to change any habit. A committed daily practice, which we'll help you develop later in this chapter, will be the most powerful tool in your arsenal for changing bad habits.

IDENTIFYING AND USING YOUR STRENGTHS

The other side of living with accountability involves being true to our best selves. Sure, the Enneagram teaches us to pinpoint and work on what's difficult for us, but it's also important to stay positive. Chugging through our daily lives and simply trying to survive, we often get settled into routines that don't always serve us. The career choices, relationships, and lifestyles we choose aren't always in accordance with our strengths, and don't always allow us to tap into our most powerful gifts. Too often, we make our choices around what gives us immediate satisfaction, doing what someone else thought would be good for us, or simply because we've always done things this way and change hasn't occurred to us.

Learning the Enneagram is frequently a happy experience. Discovering our type gives us a clear road map to our deepest essential qualities and gifts—qualities we may have seen in our lives but haven't been able to put our finger on completely. These qualities are broad. For example, there are many ways one can embody essential strength. We have endless possibilities for creating a life where we can embody these strong core abilities. Cultivating your Enneagram type's highest gifts can be done in any kind of life circumstances.

Even so, it takes work to create a life that feels deeply aligned to your inner self, especially if you, like many of us, haven't always made choices that are in service of your personal path and are looking at making significant life changes to correct these. In the earlier chapters of this book, we've discussed the healthy, high-level qualities of each type, as well as the strengths your type possesses in careers and intimate relationships—strengths that can be individualized to your own situation. To discover your own ideal life path, some deep self-examination is in order.

To start, look at your life as it is now. For example:

▶ What is your living situation?

▶ What are your most important relationships?

▶ What is your career path?

▶ What are your hobbies and interests outside of work?

▶ Are you satisfied with your life as it is in the present?

It's common to have aspects of your life that you really enjoy and others that you want to change. For example, you may love your profession, but have a difficult time getting along with your boss, or not like the city where your job is located. Or perhaps you're a high-energy person in a low-energy job or family, but you make up for it by volunteering many hours at a high-impact organization. Make two columns in a journal or word processing document with the following titles: What about my life feels aligned with me? What feels off course?

To work on making a vision of a deeply aligned life, along with considering your Enneagram type's gifts, think about the feedback you've gotten from your loved ones and in the workplace. It's common for themes to emerge. Perhaps numerous bosses have complimented you on your impeccable paperwork, or your family members notice how well you comfort the young children in your extended family. Consider, as well, what you dreamed about as a young child, and what activities you truly enjoy. Perhaps you really love going to the theater or leading meetings. All of these provide hints for discovering and following your strengths.

As you work on identifying your strengths and creating a life that uses them, keep the following things in mind:

Using your gifts is about empowering yourself. The best goals are ones that are completely in our control. Wanting our loved ones or our coworkers to change will only lead to disappointment. They need to live their own lives and make their own choices.

Your life path may be different than the advice you get from your parents, friends, or even your mentors. Deep personal inquiry is the best way to get these kinds of answers, and our own clear, present, inner knowing is our best guide.

A deeply aligned life will be fulfilling on many levels, but it doesn't always create instant happiness. All of us have ups and downs and unpredictable forks in the road that we don't expect. As the old chestnut says, "Life is what happens when we're busy making other plans." The good news is this: we can still embody our highest selves and best qualities, *and* be walking our highest path, in an unpredictable world.

Developing a Daily Growth Practice

In addition to observing your habits and self-talk and bringing your life into alignment with your strengths, another key way to build a foundation of personal growth is to develop a daily practice. In order to grow and change, you can benefit from the consistency that a daily practice brings. Like building muscle at the gym, a daily practice strengthens the inner observer every day and is easily integrated into your everyday routine.

The idea of adding a daily practice into your busy life can be intimidating to those who are just starting out. The good news is that it doesn't have to be scary. Especially when you're first starting out, a daily practice can be brief. Even a practice of just a few minutes first thing in the morning every day will help you develop self-awareness and presence! A personal practice should be something you look forward to doing, so you're more likely to stick to it.

Here are some suggestions for daily practices:

Keep a journal. Many Enneagram books include inquiry questions specific to your type that you can journal about. We've included some questions in the Appendix (page 157) as a starting point for inquiry. You can also find general thought-provoking questions in spiritually oriented Enneagram books and other books about spirituality. If you prefer an approach that is less structured, writing about whatever is on your mind will help you gain clarity into yourself and purge negative thoughts and emotions.

Meditate. Experienced meditators may meditate for long periods of time, but you can benefit from practicing for 10 minutes a day. Make sure to find a position that's comfortable for you, and don't worry if you experience a "monkey mind"—an unsettled, restless, distracted mind that hops about among thoughts and topics—while you meditate. The thoughts and feelings that arise in this space will teach you a lot about yourself. Just remember to breathe through it!

Create art. If you're a highly visual person, you may love drawing or painting every day and seeing what symbolism arises in your work—and how you feel as you create it. If you're a musician, try consciously playing or singing a simple note or scale. Expressive dance is another wonderful creative practice, particularly for a kinesthetically oriented artist.

Move your body. Physical movement is another great practice, especially if you tend to feel ungrounded and out of touch with your body. Conscious walking, stretching, yoga, or other deliberate movement allows a great space for your true self to emerge.

Most importantly, find a practice that works for you! Aim to find a practice that you find engaging and fun. Don't be afraid to play around with different practices until you find one that sticks.

THREE CENTERS
GUIDED MEDITATION

If you like, you can use a guided meditation like this one to get in touch with the energy and intelligence of all three Centers:

As you take a deep breath in and let it out, feel your feet on the floor. Sense the solidness and strength of your body. Notice any areas of discomfort and breathe into them. Notice the boundary where your body ends and the world begins.

Move into the space in your heart, pulling your shoulders back with a deep breath and letting your chest open. Breathe and feel any emotions that are there. Let them move through you. Breathe into this connection with yourself.

Take another deep breath, in and out, and notice what's happening in your mind. Let thoughts come and go, and see that there's a part of you holding and observing them. Notice the spaciousness and clarity that are there to support you when your mind is still.

Breathe in deeply. Feel your grounded body, your open heart, and your spacious mind working together. Take another deep breath and come back to the room.

BALANCING THE CENTERS IN YOUR PRACTICE

Practices come in many forms. Some build on our natural strengths, while others bring out capacities that we usually overlook. If you're looking to bring your life into balance, consider choosing a daily practice that connects with your underdeveloped capabilities, using the Centers as a shortcut.

Remember the Enneagram's three Centers from chapter 1? The Gut Center (dominant for Types One, Eight, and Nine) brings somatic intelligence, grounding, and action. The Heart Center (dominant for Types Two, Three, and Four) offers a sense of identity, connection, and emotional intelligence. The Head Center (dominant for Types Five,

Six, and Seven) encompasses clarity, critical thinking, and guidance. We possess the intelligences of all three Centers, but we tend to be most comfortable and well-versed in our own type's "home base."

Just as we have a dominant Center, we also have one that we access least often. (See *Understanding the Enneagram*, listed in the Resource section on page 161, for further reading. It's the source of the Centers theory we use throughout the book.) Unlike our dominant Center, our underused Center is relatively free from our personality's agenda. We don't think about it much at all, and we often feel uncomfortable when we consider engaging with it. Because its abilities are so different from our usual picture of ourselves, they bring enormous potential for freedom and balance. This makes our underused Center a wonderful guide for creating growth practices. As we work with this Center, we develop new abilities and get a nice "break" from our typical way of doing things. We feel more relaxed, centered, and whole. Here are some ideas for using your least-accessed Center to balance out your life. Keep them in mind as you choose a daily practice.

TYPES FOUR, FIVE, AND NINE UNDERUSE THE GUT CENTER

These types tend to focus first and foremost on their thoughts and feelings. They may get up and move around, but they tend to resist feeling the full weight and physicality of their bodies. Here are ideas for practices to help these types get grounded:

- Maintaining an exercise routine

- Participating in movement-based practices, such as tai chi, yoga, or walking meditation

- Consciously feeling the weight of your legs and feet as you go about your day

- Deep breathing and breath-based meditation

- Taking action on something you've been putting off

TYPES THREE, SEVEN, AND EIGHT UNDERUSE THE HEART CENTER

These types are often quite busy and focus on their physical bodies and thoughts. They frequently resist feeling their feelings and emotional needs at the expense of running around and getting things done. Here are some practices to help these types connect with their feelings and true selves:

▶ Taking daily quiet time to connect with yourself

▶ Journaling

▶ Taking part in compassion-based practices, such as loving-kindness meditation—a type of meditation where you send good wishes to other people

▶ Expressing gratitude to others or keeping a gratitude log

▶ Sharing your feelings with someone you trust

TYPES ONE, TWO, AND SIX UNDERUSE THE HEAD CENTER

These types feel a strong sense of duty and use their feelings and physical bodies to meet their responsibilities. These types may be highly intelligent, but they focus on standards and rules at the expense of pursuing their ideas. The following practices can help these types step back from commitments and clear their minds:

▶ Meditating

▶ Reading and researching topics of interest

▶ Following curiosity rather than an agenda

▶ Debating and discussing ideas

▶ Doing daily chores or actions mindfully

JULIA'S GROWTH PATH

Julia, our spirited Type Seven, is enjoying the calm that her daily meditation practice brings. She finds that taking quiet time to herself every
day slows her overall pace of life and reconnects her with a loving,
and often overlooked, Heart Center. As time goes by, she notices
herself feeling less pressure to complete projects quickly and find
exciting things to do. The more aware she is of her frenetic self-talk,
the more she tells herself that she doesn't have to seek out sources
of happiness. She experiences more joy in the here and now, even in
simple activities like cleaning or walking to the supermarket. At work,
she shows accountability to herself by engaging in projects like the
Women's Leadership Committee that satisfy her craving for variety.
The Enneagram has taught her that she values freedom and possibilities, and there's nothing wrong with holding these values. They can
be honored in ways that bring her happiness rather than indulged
through bad habits, such as buying things she doesn't truly value or
spending time on social media at work. Her boyfriend, Miguel, and
her friend Lakesha are a good support system, and she talks honestly
with both of them about the work she's doing to bring balance and
happiness into her life, the challenges she encounters with it, and the
progress she's making. She also joins some friends in a weekly meditation group.

Your personal growth path may have commonalities with Julia's,
or it may look quite different. Even if many of us are ultimately looking
for the same things in life, such as happiness, success, and balance,
the paths that will bring us to these results vary widely, and the needs
that we must meet to get there are equally diverse. The important
thing is to be true to you and find support for your own unique values
and goals.

Working Through Hard Times

When we begin to work with the Enneagram or pursue another personal or spiritual growth path, it's tempting to believe the tough times have passed us by for good. In reality, all of us have good times and difficult times in our lives, no matter how much inner work we do. Certain life experiences, positive or negative, are great equalizers in life.

Committed work with the Enneagram gives us the ability to handle the challenges life throws at us. All of us know how difficult it is to stay centered and present when we experience tragedy. When we encounter life difficulties, it's very easy to "fall off the wagon," or to end up making a series of poor choices that have a snowball effect in our lives. The good news is, we all have the potential to make grounded, compassionate, and discerning decisions under duress.

This is why Enneagram expert Russ Hudson likes to say, "Practice when it's easy so it'll be there when it's hard." Under extreme stress, people tend to fall back on old patterns, and it's extremely difficult to suddenly start doing centering practices when you don't have a history of doing them previously. When your life is generally going well (like our friend Julia—going well doesn't have to mean everything is perfect!), you have the coping skills to develop internal coping mechanisms and find external support—support that will help you cope with life when things aren't so good.

If you're picking up this book during trying times, here are some suggestions for coping:

Stick to a Routine: Regardless of Enneagram type, all of us have our stress levels increase as more changes get thrust upon us. Even if it's something as simple as continuing to get coffee at 8:30 a.m. before work, do regular rituals that support and sustain you. If you've come up with an Enneagram-based practice, or something else that supports your inner life, keep doing it even if it feels hard. It may not always feel good when we do this, but this time will allow you to check in with yourself and become more grounded and aware of what you *really* need. This is also a safe space for you to process the difficult emotions that inevitably come up in difficult times.

Rally Your Troops: John Donne famously wrote, "No man is an island." In other words, no person, regardless of gender or privilege, can get through rough times on their own, and everyone needs a team of supporters. Supportive family members, friends, and partners will be there to love and encourage you through the darkness, and provide suggestions and perspective. If you're involved in any supportive community, whether oriented toward personal growth, spirituality, or otherwise, stay involved in this group in any way you can, and don't be afraid to ask for the help you need. You'll be able to give back when your life situation has improved.

Appreciate the Impermanence of Life: It's human to want the good times in our life to remain, while hoping the difficult ones pass quickly or don't come at all. Even when we're on the right path, though, our lives will inevitably have their ups and downs. Real presence comes from simply being with whatever life throws at us, and having the courage to be radically alive with whatever happens to be unfolding. During good times, appreciate them, but know that nothing in life is permanent. During the tough times, comfort yourself in knowing that this, too, will pass.

HANDLING ADVERSITY WITH RESILIENCE

The Enneagram's way of recognizing our patterns and pointing us toward behavioral changes can help us care for ourselves when the going gets rough. Let's look at the story of Julia's boyfriend Miguel, who leaned on the Enneagram during a family health crisis.

Miguel has always been close to his mother, Esperanza. They live near each other and visit regularly. When his usually healthy, vivacious mother is diagnosed with breast cancer, he is shocked and upset. His Type Two helping instincts go into overdrive. He wants to drop his other responsibilities and spend his time caring for and supporting her.

In the past, when family members or other loved ones were in crisis, Miguel would take on the primary responsibility for their care. He offered money, took leaves from work when possible, and when he couldn't, he spent most of his evenings and weekends caretaking. He was left sleep-deprived, low on funds, and burnt out. Thanks to his work with the Enneagram, Miguel realizes that his nurturing tends to go overboard when he feels that a loved one is suffering. While he deeply values caring for his mother during her illness, he realizes that his responsibilities extend further. He has a team at work that depends on him, even if their health is not at risk. He has a relationship with Julia that requires time and care, but also offers much-needed support. Most importantly, he needs to take care of himself in order to effectively support his mother.

Miguel connects with his father and local family members, and leads them in organizing a care schedule. This creates a network of people who each take responsibility for aspects of caretaking, and ensures that responsibility doesn't fall solely on Miguel's shoulders. Miguel takes responsibility for accompanying his mother to important medical appointments, while his father ensures that she receives regular treatment at home. Miguel and his siblings take turns helping with domestic tasks, with Julia and his siblings' partners pitching in.

Maintaining his regular habits helps Miguel manage his energy and emotions while supporting his mother. In the past, he'd found it difficult to be productive at work when caretaking for a loved one, but his job now requires more responsibility and the welfare of his team often rests on his decisions. He makes sure to stick to his regular sleep and exercise schedules rather than staying up caretaking or worrying about his mother. Prior to her diagnosis, he had started meditating with Julia, and she encourages him to continue. Sitting quietly on a cushion brings Miguel into close contact with painful thoughts and feelings that he'd rather avoid. There's nowhere for him to run from them. Rather than acting strong and stoic, he often finds himself breaking down into tears. Julia sits with him and listens. Prior to the Enneagram, she would have tried to cheer him up; now, she offers support by being there for Miguel as he expresses and processes his feelings rather than pushing them aside to act.

Thanks to his foundation of self-care, Miguel's Type Two strengths of empathy and attentiveness shine through in supporting his mother through treatment. He asks her how she is doing whenever they are together, listens to her feelings, and shows love in any way he can. Rather than treating her as helpless, like he is tempted to do, he makes sure that she has primary input in her treatment. They have long conversations about the parts of life that are important to each of them. No matter what happens with her health, Miguel realizes he can offer his mother genuine, loving presence.

Toward Change

As you can see, the Enneagram is not only a powerful tool to apply to our relationships and career, but a way for us to do deep inner work and create powerful, long-lasting change. By making one small change in our actions or perspective at a time, all of us will step into awareness and presence. Present, radical change isn't always easy, but deep self-compassion and commitment to our inner work allows us to move with the flow of life, rather than fighting against it. We all have a meaningful path in our lives that exists for us to discover and follow.

CONCLUSION

Throughout this book, we've covered some basics of Enneagram theory and explored applications for the system—applications that range from career choice to dating to toughing out life's rough patches. In writing about these applications, we hoped to give you a toolbox to help with the daily challenges you face. In our experience, there's no substitute for the Enneagram as a shortcut to self-awareness. Once you discover your type, you uncover previously hidden motivations behind your behavior. You come face to face with what you want, unearth the ineffective strategies that your ego uses to chase that desire, and start to think about ways to fulfill this craving that are different from your ordinary habits. The journey is both sobering and illuminating.

The Enneagram is a wonderful tool, but a tool is only as good as the purposes it's used for. As you discern the types of other people in your life, you can use the Enneagram to navigate interactions, being mindful of your own biases and tailoring communication to their goals and perspectives. You can introduce the system to groups, creating a common language for members to understand each other. (Make sure to frame it as a tool rather than a way of defining people; most of us don't want to be "put in a box.") As you learn about yourself, you may find inspiration in designing a life that best fits your needs and brings your gifts into the world. The most fruitful applications of the Enneagram come from using it for growth. Observe the ways your personality's desires shape your actions. Notice when its self-talk is monopolizing your attention, taking you out of the moment, and preventing you from fully engaging. Use these moments of observation as a wake-up call to return your attention to the world around you and make active, conscious choices. It's up to you to take what you've learned from the Enneagram and apply it in the ways that best fit your personal needs and circumstances.

We encourage you to continue your Enneagram journey beyond these pages. This book is just the tip of the iceberg when it comes to the insights the Enneagram has to offer. Take your time learning about the nine personality types and finding your own. If it's feasible for you, explore the Enneagram in person through a workshop, conference, or training. Read about the areas that you'd like to use the Enneagram for, whether they're parenting, business, or spiritual growth. Learn about additional aspects of the theory that interest you. Riso and Hudson's theory of the Levels of Development, mentioned in chapter 1 (page 14), and the Instincts/Subtypes theory proposed by Naranjo and expanded on by other teachers, are rich areas for self-exploration beyond the scope of introductory theory. In the Resources section in the back of this book, we've listed a few recommendations out of the many sources available for deepening your Enneagram knowledge.

The more you learn about the Enneagram, the deeper your understanding, and the more tools you will have at your disposal for navigating the highs and lows of life. It's hard to go back once you've seen your patterns and motivations clearly. Your misconceptions about who you are fall away and a new, more deliberate way of living becomes possible. We hope that discovering the Enneagram brings you as much clarity and guidance as it's brought to us!

SHORTCUTS FOR BREAKING OUT OF YOUR BOX

The following questions and practices interrupt your type's usual way of seeing and engaging with the world. We're sharing them in order to give you new ways of looking at things and open up possibilities. Use them as a jump-start for living in a more balanced way.

TYPE ONE

QUESTIONS

Is this my responsibility alone, or are there ways I can find help and support?

What do I want to do that's fun, and how can I make it happen?

PRACTICE

Break a rule or principle. It doesn't have to be major, but it should be something that pushes your limits. Choose something you believe you shouldn't do, and do it. Notice what the experience is like.

TYPE TWO

QUESTIONS

What do I need right now?

How can I show care for myself the way I do for my loved ones?

PRACTICE

Take a "helping vacation." Set aside a stretch of time (longer than is comfortable for you) when you won't check in with or help anyone. Say "no" if asked. Pay attention to what feelings and needs arise in you.

TYPE THREE

QUESTIONS

What would I do with my time if no one was watching me?

What connects me with my heart?

PRACTICE

Unplug. Set aside a period when you won't answer the phone, check e-mail, post on social media, or otherwise see, share, or answer any messages. Tune in to yourself and reflect on any insights that come up.

TYPE FOUR

QUESTIONS

What are the realistic desires behind my fantasies, and what steps can I take to make them come true?

What can I do right now to bring goodness into the world?

PRACTICE

Engage with the world around you. Choose a productive activity that involves other people and commit to doing it for a set period of time. Notice the abilities that you show as you take action rather than living in your head.

TYPE FIVE

QUESTIONS

Do I actually need to know more about this, or can I get started and learn as I go along?

What can I do to feel connected right now?

PRACTICE

Start something. Choose an idea or project that you've been thinking about and begin step one: no research or deliberation allowed. Schedule time to complete steps 2, 3, etc. What's it like to act without overthinking?

TYPE SIX

QUESTIONS

What decision feels right to me?

What would I do if I weren't afraid, and how can I do it anyway?

PRACTICE

Choose a situation you're on the fence about. If you were the authority, what would you advise yourself to do? Have a talk with your "inner guide," and implement their advice. Consult this guide whenever you want input on something.

TYPE SEVEN

QUESTIONS

What do I enjoy about what I'm doing or where I am right now?

Which of my ideas is worth focusing on?

PRACTICE

Out of many possible activities, choose one that holds meaning for you. Commit to doing it for a set period of time. If you start thinking about something else, remind yourself of the activity's intrinsic meaning.

TYPE EIGHT

QUESTIONS

What support do I need from others, and how can I receive it?

How can I show caring toward the people who mean a lot to me?

PRACTICE

Do something relaxing for a set period of time. Choose an activity that's quiet and reflective rather than stimulating. Use the time to connect with yourself and your heart. What's it like to take a break from expending energy?

TYPE NINE

QUESTIONS

How do I want to be seen in the world, and how can I shine right now?

Is this a situation where I'm truly fine with any outcome, or do I have an opinion?

PRACTICE

Identify something you want and speak up about it. Ask for help if possible. If it's an action you want to take or a project you want to do, determine and initiate the first steps. What's it like to rock the boat rather than smoothing the waters?

RESOURCES

RECOMMENDED BOOKS AND WEBSITES

The Complete Enneagram: 27 Paths to Greater Self-Knowledge, by Beatrice Chestnut

Enneagram in the Narrative Tradition. www.enneagramworldwide.com

The Enneagram Institute. www.enneagraminstitute.com

The Enneagram Made Easy: Discover the 9 Types of People, by Elizabeth Wagele and Renee Baron

Enneagram Spectrum of Personality Styles, by Jerry Wagner

The Enneagram: Understanding Yourself and the Others in Your Life, by Helen Palmer

The Essential Enneagram: The Definitive Personality Test and Self-Discovery Guide, by David Daniels and Virginia Price

Understanding the Enneagram: The Practical Guide to Personality Types, by Don Riso and Russ Hudson

The Wisdom of the Enneagram: The Complete Guide to Psychological and Spiritual Growth, by Don Riso and Russ Hudson

BUSINESS AND CAREER

Awareness to Action: The Enneagram, Emotional Intelligence, and Change, by Robert Tallon and Mario Sikora

Bringing Out the Best in Yourself in Work: How to Use The Enneagram For Success, by Ginger Lapid-Bogda

The Career Within You: How to Find the Perfect Job for Your Personality, by Elizabeth Wagele and Ingrid Staff

PERSONAL GROWTH

Deep Living: Transforming Your Relationship To Everything That Matters Through The Enneagram, by Roxanne Howe-Murphy

My Best Self: Using the Enneagram to Free the Soul, by Kathleen Hurley and Theodore Dodson

Personality Types, by Don Riso and Russ Hudson

RELATIONSHIPS

Are You My Type, Am I Yours? Relationships Made Easy Through The Enneagram, by Elizabeth Wagele and Renee Baron

The Enneagram in Love and Work: Understanding Your Intimate and Business Relationships, by Helen Palmer

Sex, Love, and Your Personality: The 9 Faces of Intimacy, by Mona Coates and Judith Searle

Understand Yourself, Understanding Your Partner: The Essential Enneagram Guide to a Better Relationship, by Jennifer P. Schneider and Ron Corn

SPIRITUAL GROWTH

Facets of Unity: The Enneagram of Holy Ideas, by A. H. Almaas

From Fixation to Freedom: The Enneagram of Liberation, by Eli Jaxon-Bear

The Enneagram: A Christian Perspective, by Richard Rohr and Andreas Ebert

Enneagram Transformations, by Don Riso

The Road Back to You: An Enneagram Journey to Self-Discovery, by Ian Morgan Cron and Suzanne Stabile

The Spiritual Dimension of the Enneagram: Nine Faces of the Soul, by Sandra Maitri

The Wisdom of the Enneagram: The Complete Guide to Psychological and Spiritual Growth, by Don Riso and Russ Hudson

PARENTING AND YOUTH

The Enneagram for Teens: Discover Your True Personality Type and Celebrate Your True Self, by Elizabeth Wagele

The Enneagram of Parenting: The 9 Types of Children and How to Raise Them Successfully, by Elizabeth Wagele

ENNEAGRAM TESTS

Essential Enneagram Online Test, by David Daniels and Virginia Price. www.enneagramworldwide.com. Cost: $10

EnneaApp Personality Test, by Ginger Lapid-Bogda, PhD. Download for iPhone or Android at www.enneaapp.com. Cost: $3.99

Enneagram test using Integrative Intelligent Questionnaire Technology, by Dirk Cloete. integrative.co.za. Cost: $15

The RHETI, by Don Riso and Russ Hudson. www.enneagraminstitute. com. Cost: $10

The WEPSS, by Jerry Wagner, PhD. www.wepss.com. Cost: $10

REFERENCES

Beesing, Maria, Robert J. Nogosek, and Patrick H. O'Leary. *The Enneagram: A Journey of Self-Discovery*. Denville, NJ: Dimension Books, 1984.

Bell, Melanie, and Kacie Berghoef. Berghoef & Bell Innovations. Accessed November 5th, 2016. www.berghoefbell.com.

Bell, Melanie, and Kacie Berghoef. *Decoding Personality in the Workplace*. San Francisco: Berghoef & Bell Innovations, 2015.

Chernick Fauvre, Katherine, and David Fauvre. "The Enneagram 'Tritype': Exploring the Hierarchy of Your Three Centers of Intelligence." Presentation, International Enneagram Association Global Conference 2008, Atlanta, GA, August 2, 2008.

Chestnut, Beatrice. *The Complete Enneagram: 27 Paths to Greater Self-Knowledge*. Berkeley, CA: She Writes Press, 2013.

Coates, Mona, and Judith Searle. *Sex, Love, and Your Personality: The 9 Faces of Intimacy*. Santa Monica, CA: Therapy Options Press, 2011.

Condon, Tom. The Changeworks. Accessed September 8th, 2016. www.thechangeworks.com.

Daniels, David N., and Virginia Ann Price. *The Essential Enneagram: The Definitive Personality Test and Self-Discovery Guide*. New York: HarperOne, 2000.

Dash, Barbara, and Richard Dash. "Use of the Enneagram in Deepening Your Relational Communications." Presentation, International Enneagram Association Global Conference 2016, Minneapolis, MN, July 23, 2016.

The Enneagram Institute. Accessed October 12th, 2016. www.enneagraminstitute.com/

Levine, Janet. *The Enneagram Intelligences: Understanding Personality for Effective Teaching and Learning.* Westport, CT: Bergin & Garvey, 1999.

Naranjo, Claudio. *Character and Neurosis: An Integrative View.* Nevada City, CA: Gateways/IDHHB, 1994.

Olesek, Susan. Enneagram Prison Project. Accessed in 2016. www.enneagramprisonproject.org.

Ouspensky, P. D. *In Search of the Miraculous.* New York: Harcourt, Brace, 1949.

Paes, Uranio. "Endnote Address." Presentation, International Enneagram Association Global Conference 2015, Burlingame, CA, August 2, 2015.

Palmer, Helen. *The Enneagram in Love and Work: Understanding Your Intimate and Business Relationships.* San Francisco: HarperSanFrancisco, 1995.

Palmer, Helen. *The Enneagram: Understanding Yourself and the Others in Your Life.* San Francisco: HarperSanFrancisco, 1991.

Richardson, Cheryl. "Self-Care and the Enneagram." Lecture, Enneagram Global Summit 2015, Online, June 3-5, 2015.

Riso, Don Richard, and Russ Hudson. *The Enneagram Institute Training Program.* 2008-2013.

Riso, Don Richard, and Russ Hudson. *Personality Types: Using the Enneagram for Self-Discovery.* New York: Houghton Mifflin, 1996.

Riso, Don Richard, and Russ Hudson, with Paula Warner. *The Riso-Hudson Enneagram Workshop ResourceBook.* Stone Ridge, NY: The Enneagram Institute, 2010.

Riso, Don Richard, and Russ Hudson. *Understanding the Enneagram: The Practical Guide to Personality Types.* New York: Houghton Mifflin, 2000.

Riso, Don Richard, and Russ Hudson. *The Wisdom of the Enneagram: The Complete Guide to Psychological and Spiritual Growth for the Nine Personality Types*. New York: Bantam Books, 1999.

Sikora, Mario, and Maria Jose Munita. *Awareness to Action International Certification Program Level 1*. Burlingame, CA, 2015.

Siudzinski, Robert M., and Robert A. Siudzinski. "The Use of the Enneagram in Higher Education: Powerful Insights for Young Adult Learning, Career Crafting, and Community Engagement." Presentation, International Enneagram Association Global Conference 2014, Burlingame, CA, July 25, 2014.

Tallon, Robert, and Mario Sikora. *Awareness to Action: The Enneagram, Emotional Intelligence, and Change*. Scranton, PA: University of Scranton Press, 2004.

Wagele, Elizabeth, and Ingrid Stabb. *The Career Within You: How to Find the Perfect Job for Your Personality*. New York: HarperOne, 2009.

Wagele, Elizabeth. *The Enneagram of Parenting: The 9 Types of Children and How to Raise Them Successfully*. New York: HarperOne, 1997.

INDEX

A

accountability, living with, 139–145
activism, career in, 97
adaptable performers, work
  environment, 84–85
addiction support, career in, 101
administrative professionals, 93, 101
adventure in relationships, 122–123
adversity, handing with
  resilience, 152–154
advocate, career as, 101
analyst, career as, 99
animal professionals, 107
architect, career as, 99
arrows in Enneagram
  and careers, 98
  explained, 17
  movement along, 70
art, creating, 146
artistic professions, 100
Assertive social style, 20
  Julia's case study, 68
  at work, 90
assistant, career as, 103
athletic professions, 95–96, 107
Attachment Triad, 24
authenticity in relationships, 117–118

B

bad habits, recognizing and
  changing, 141–143
balance, increasing internal
  sense of, 138
Beesing, Maria, 14
body
  and instinct, 19
  moving, 146
Bonaparte, Napoleon, 105
Branson, Richard, 103
Brokaw, Tom, 93
Bush, George H. W., 101
business professionals, 94, 99, 104

C

campaigner, career as, 103
careers. See also generalist
  professionals; professions
  arrows, 98
  interests and abilities, 98
  Type Eights, 104–105
  Type Fives, 98–100
  Type Fours, 96–97
  Type Nines, 105–107
  Type Ones, 91–93
  Type Sevens, 102–104
  Type Sixes, 100–102
  Type Threes, 94–96
  Type Twos, 93–94
  wings, 98
Centers
  balancing in practice, 147–148
  guided meditation, 147
  Gut, 18–19, 148
  Head, 18–19, 68, 149
  Heart, 18–19, 149
CEO or executive, career as, 104
change and growth, facilitating, 136–137.
  See also dynamism and change
"chief feature," identifying, 13
child development and education, 93
children, working with, 103, 107
circle of unity, 15
clarity, seeking, 42–44
coach, career as, 96
colleagues, communicating with, 90
communication
  with colleagues, 90
  and media career, 95, 102
  styles, 127–129
community organizer, career as, 106
compassionate creators,
  work environment, 85
compatibility, busting myths about, 117
Competency Types, 22, 126
Compliant Types, 21, 90

Conflict Resolution styles
  explained, 22–23
  Julia's case study, 68–69
  in relationships, 126–127
conflicts at work, 90
connection, seeking, 33–35
consulting experts, 27
Cooperators at work, 90
coping skills, improving, 138
creative professions, 100, 106
Curie, Marie, 99
customer service, career in, 94

D

daily growth practice,
  developing, 145–146
Daniels, David, 14, 26, 65
dating fears, overcoming, 111.
  See also relationships
Depp, Johnny, 97
designer, career as, 96–97
Diana, Princess of Wales, 101
director, career as, 102
doers in work environment, 88–89
Donne, John, 152
dynamism and change, hexad of,
  16. See also change and growth

E

Earhart, Amelia, 103
early childhood professionals, 107
education. See also instructor;
  professor; teacher
  career in, 91, 100
  and child development, 93
egalitarians in work environment, 86–87
Eights' qualities. See also Type Eights
  diagram, 52
  healthy and average, 51, 53
  security point, 52
  seeking power, 51–53
  stress point, 52
  wings and arrows, 52–53
  work environment, 88–89
emotional depth in
  relationships, 118–119

Emotional Realness Types
  conflict resolution in
    relationships, 126
  explained, 23
empathetic connectors
  described, 33
  work environment, 83–84
engineer, career as, 99–100
The Enneagram, 14
Enneagram
  arrows, 17
  authors, 14
  benefits, 11, 136–137
  circle of unity, 15
  contemporary status, 14–15
  function of, 8
  growth paths, 8–9
  hexad of dynamism and
    change, 16
  historical roots, 11, 13
  Integration Point, 17
  nine points, 15
  numbers of personality types, 16
  Security Points, 17
  Stress Points, 17
  structure, 15–16
  triangle of dynamic interaction, 15
  uses of, 9
  using, 137
The Enneagram Institute, 14–15
*The Enneagram: Understanding
  Yourself and Others in Your Life*, 14
entertainer, career as, 95, 103
entrepreneur, career as, 97, 102, 104
event planning and executing,
  career in, 103
executive coach, career as, 104
executive or CEO, career as, 104
exercising, 146
experts, consulting, 27
explorers, work environment, 87–88

F

family relationships and roles, 129–133
feedback, getting from
  family and friends, 27

financial industry, career
in, 92, 100, 106
first responder, career as, 101
fitness professionals, 105
Fives' qualities. *See also* Type Fives
diagram, 43
healthy and average, 42
security point, 43
seeking clarity, 42–44
stress point, 43
unhealthy, wings, and
arrows, 43–44
work environment, 86
founding thinkers, 64
Fours' qualities. *See also*
Type Fours
diagram, 40
healthy and average, 39
Julia's case study, 80–81
security point, 40
seeking identity, 39
self-knowledge, 39
stress point, 40
unhealthy, wings, and
arrows, 40–41
work environment, 85
freedom, seeking, 48–50
Frustration style, 25, 69

G

Gates, Bill, 99
generalist professionals,
102. *See also* careers
goals, setting, 144–145
Goldberg, Whoopi, 106
goodness, desire for, 30
Gore, Al, 92
government, career in, 100
growth
and change, 136–137
developing daily practice,
145–146
growth path for Julia, 150
guidance, seeking, 45–47
guided meditation, using, 147
Gurdjieff, G. I., 13, 64

Gut Center
explained, 18–19
underuse, 148

H

habits, recognizing and
changing, 141–143
hard times, working through, 151–154
harmony, seeking, 54–56
Head Center
explained, 18–19
Julia's case study, 68
underuse, 149
health professionals, 92, 97
healthcare industry, career in, 93
Heart Center
explained, 18–19
underuse, 149
helping professions, 103
hexad of dynamism and change, 16
historian, career as, 106
home organization, career in, 92
Hornevian Triads, 20
hospitality industry, career in, 93, 103
Hudson, Russ, 20, 65, 136, 151
human resources professionals, 95
humanitarian work, career in, 97

I

Ichazo, Oscar, 13, 29, 64
identity
seeking, 39–41
and values, 19
image consultant, career as, 96
impact, having, 51
impactful doers, work
environment, 88–89
impermanence of life,
appreciating, 152
Initiators at work, 90
innovative specialists, work
environment, 86
instincts and bodies, 19
instructor, career as, 98. *See also*
education; professor; teacher
Integration Point, 17

Integrative Enneagram Solutions, 26
integrity, seeking, 30–32
intellectual depth in
  relationships, 120–121
Islam, Sufism branch of, 13

J

Joan of Arc, 92
jobs. *See* work environment
journal, keeping, 145–146
Julia's case study. *See also* Miguel's
  case study; Sevens' qualities
    Assertive social style, 68
    becoming whole self, 76
    Conflict Resolution style, 68–69
    daily life, 74
    expectations of Enneagram, 63
    Frustration style, 69
    growth path, 150
    Head Center, 68
    navigating family
      dynamics, 131–133
    Object Relations style, 69
    Positive Outlook style, 68–69
    practical applications, 71–74
    relationships, 62–63, 72–74
    Six Wing, 67
    solving problems at work, 80–82
    Type Seven, 65–67
    work, 61–63, 71–72

K

Kabbalistic Tree of Life, 29
Kennedy Onassis, Jackie, 97
King, Martin Luther, Jr., 104
knowing and support, obtaining, 19
knowledge, importance
  to Type Fives, 42

L

Lapid-Bogda, Ginger, 27
leadership positions, 104–105
legal mediator, career as, 106
legal system, career in, 91
Letterman, David, 102

life, appreciating impermanence
  of, 152
London, Stacey, 96
love. *See* relationships

M

management consultant, career as, 99
manager, career as, 97, 104, 106
marketing
    and recruiting career, 97
    and sales career, 95, 102
media and communication,
  career in, 102
mediator in work environment, 89
meditating, 146–147
meeting people, 112–113
mental health support, career in, 101
Miguel's case study, 152–154.
    See also Julia's case study
military and police, careers in, 101, 105
mindfulness, 139
ministry, career in, 92, 94, 101
motivational speaker, career as, 96, 104
movers and shakers in
  relationships, 123–124

N

Naranjo, Claudio, 13–14, 64
Narrative Tradition, 14, 26
networker, career as, 94
Nightingale, Florence, 93
nine, significance of, 29
Nines' qualities. *See also* Type Nines
    healthy and average, 54
    security point, 55
    seeking harmony, 54–56
    stress point, 55
    unhealthy, wings, and
      arrows, 55–56
    work environment, 89
"No man is an island," 152
Nogosek, Robert, 14
nonprofits, career in, 91
nuances, understanding, 70
numbers of personality types, 16

O

Object Relations style
  explained, 24–25
  Julia's case study, 69
O'Leary, Patrick, 14
Ones' qualities. *See also* Type Ones
  healthy and average, 30
  Julia's case study, 80–81
  security point, 31
  stress point, 31
  unhealthy, wings, and
    arrows, 31–32
  work environment, 82–83
outdoor occupations, 106

P

Palmer, Helen, 14, 65
peace and unity in
  relationships, 124–125
people, meeting, 112–113
perfectionists, work
  environment, 82–83
performer, career as, 95–96, 102
Perry, Katy, 104
personal development, 136
personal identity and values, 19
personal value, sense of, 36
personality types. *See also* typing tests
  number of, 29
  numbers associated with, 16
  variations, 28–29
  wings, 28–29
Personality Types, 14
physical instincts and bodies, 19
pilot, career as, 105
Plotinus, 29
police and military, careers in, 101
politics, careers in, 92, 95, 104
Positive Outlook Types
  conflict resolution in
    relationships, 126
  explained, 23
  Julia's case study, 68–69
possibility, pursuit of, 48
power, seeking, 51–53

practical applications, Julia's
  case study, 71–74
Price, Virginia, 26
principles, motivation by, 30
professional advocates, 101
professions, high-visibility in,
  95. *See also* careers
professor, career as, 98. *See also*
  education; instructor; teacher
project management, career in, 101
property-related professions, 105
psychological insights, 13–14
public information provider,
  career as, 99
public relations, career in, 95
public safety and service,
  career in, 105

Q

quality assurance, career in, 92, 101

R

Reagan, Ronald, 106
Rejection Triad, 25
relationship counselor, career as, 94
relationships. *See also* dating fears
  adventure, 122–123
  authenticity, 117–118
  bonding, 115–116
  conflict resolution, 126–127
  emotional depth, 118–119
  high ideals, 114–115
  improving, 139
  intellectual depth, 120–121
  Julia's case study, 72–74
  movers and shakers, 123–124
  peace and unity, 124–125
  strengthening, 131
  support and direction, 121–122
  Type Eights, 123–124
  Type Fives, 120–121
  Type Fours, 118–119
  Type Nines, 124–125
  Type Ones, 114–115
  Type Sevens, 122–123
  Type Sixes, 121–122

Relationships (*continued*)
Type Threes, 117–118
Type Twos, 115–116
religious occupations, 92, 94, 101
remote work, career in, 100
researcher, career as, 96, 99–100
RHETI (Riso-Hudson Enneagram
Type Indicator), 26
Rice, Anne, 97
Riso, Don, 14, 20, 65, 97, 136
Robbins, Tony, 96
Roberts, Julia, 102
Romney, Mitt, 95
routine, sticking to, 151

S

sales and marketing, career in, 95, 102
Sandberg, Sheryl, 104
scientific professions, 92, 100, 106
security guard, career as, 105
Security Points, 17
self, healing, 138
self-awareness, benefits, 138–139
self-discovery, embracing,
57. *See also* whole self
self-knowledge
desire for, 39
vs. test results, 27
sensitivity, 39
Seven Deadly Sins, 29
Sevens' qualities. *See also* Julia's
case study; Type Sevens
diagram, 49
healthy and average, 48
security point, 49
seeking freedom, 48–50
stress point, 49
unhealthy, wings, and
arrows, 49–50
work environment, 87–88
Simmons, Richard, 93
Six Wing, Julia's case study, 67
Sixes' qualities. *See also* Type Sixes
diagram, 46
healthy and average, 45
security point, 46
seeking guidance, 45–47

stress point, 46
unhealthy, wings, and arrows, 46–47
work environment, 86–87
social justice, career in, 91
social styles, 20–21
Soloists at work, 90
spiritual application, 75
startup founder, career as, 100
Stewart, Martha, 93
strengths, identifying and
using, 143–145
Stress Points, 17
Sufism, 13
support
and direction in relationships,
121–122
getting during trying times, 152
and knowing, 19
survival strategies, 25
Swift, Taylor, 95

T

tax professionals, 92
teacher, career as, 97. *See also*
education; instructor; professor
technical professions, 98, 106
test taking, 26–27
therapeutic professionals, 93, 97, 107
thought leader, career as, 99
three Centers guided meditation, 147
Threes' qualities. *See also* Type Threes
diagram, 37
healthy and average, 36
Julia's case study, 81
personal sense of value, 36
security point, 37
seeking value, 36–38
stress point, 37
unhealthy, wings, and
arrows, 37–38
work environment, 84–85
travel-related professions, 103
triads
Assertive, 20
Attachment, 24
Competency, 22
Compliant, 21

Emotional Realness, 23
explained, 18
Frustration, 25
look-alikes, 70
Positive Outlook, 23
Rejection, 25
Withdrawn, 21
triangle of dynamic interaction, 15
truck driver, career as, 105
trying times, working through,
  151–154
Twos' qualities. *See also* Type Twos
diagram, 34
healthy and average, 33
Julia's case study, 73
security point, 34
seeking connection, 33–35
seeking integrity, 30
stress point, 34
unhealthy, wings, and
  arrows, 34–35
work environment, 83–84
Type Eights. *See also* Eights' qualities
careers, 104–105
changing bad habits, 142
communication style, 129
family relationships and roles, 130
meeting people, 113
relationships, 123–124
underuse of Heart Center, 149
Type Fives. *See also* Fives' qualities
careers, 98–100
changing bad habits, 142
communication style, 128
family relationships and roles, 130
meeting people, 113
relationships, 120–121
underuse of Gut Center, 148
Type Fours. *See also* Fours' qualities
careers, 96–97
changing bad habits, 142
communication style, 128
family relationships and roles, 130
meeting people, 112
relationships, 118–119
underuse of Gut Center, 148

Type Nines. *See also* Nines' qualities
careers, 105–107
changing bad habits, 142
communication style, 129
family relationships and roles, 130
meeting people, 113
relationships, 124–125
underuse of Gut Center, 148
Type Ones. *See also* Ones' qualities
careers, 91–93
changing bad habits, 141
communication style, 127–128
family relationships and roles, 130
meeting people, 112
underuse of Head Center, 149
Type Sevens. *See also* Sevens' qualities
careers, 102–104
changing bad habits, 142
communication style, 129
family relationships and roles, 130
meeting people, 113
relationships, 122–123
underuse of Heart Center, 149
Type Sixes. *See also* Sixes' qualities
careers, 100–102
changing bad habits, 142
communication style, 128–129
family relationships and roles, 130
meeting people, 113
relationships, 121–122
underuse of Head Center, 149
Type Threes. *See also* Threes' qualities
careers, 94–96
changing bad habits, 141–142
communication style, 128
family relationships and roles, 130
meeting people, 112
relationships, 117–118
underuse of Heart Center, 149
Type Twos. *See also* Twos' qualities
careers, 93–94
changing bad habits, 141
communication style, 128
family relationships and roles, 130
meeting people, 112
underuse of Head Center, 149

typing tests, 26–27. *See also* personality types

U

unity, circle of, 15

V

value
  authenticity of, 36
  and identity, 19

W

Wagner, Jerry, 26
whole self, becoming, 76.
  See also self-discovery
"Why," considering, 70
Williams, Robin, 104
Williams, Serena, 105
wings
  and careers, 98
  explained, 28–29
Withdrawn Types
  explained, 21
  at work, 90

work environment
  adaptable performers, 84–85
  committed egalitarians, 86–87
  compassionate creators, 85
  easygoinig mediators, 89
  Eights' qualities, 88–89
  empathetic connectors, 83–84
  energetic explorers, 87–88
  Fives' qualities, 86
  Fours' qualities, 85
  impactful doers, 88–89
  innovative specialists, 86
  Julia's case study, 71–72
  Nines' qualities, 89
  Ones' qualities, 82–83
  perfectionists, 82–83
  Sevens' qualities, 87–88
  Sixes' qualities, 86–87
  solving problems in, 80–82
  Threes' qualities, 84–85
  Twos' qualities, 83–84
writer, career as, 96, 99

ACKNOWLEDGMENTS

We would like to thank the late Don Riso and Russ Hudson, for introducing and teaching us the intricacies of the Enneagram as a tool for inner work. Our gratitude goes out also to The Enneagram Institute faculty and staff—Lynda Roberts, Gayle Scott, Michael Naylor, Brian Taylor, Katy Taylor, Donna Teresi, Jen Jeglinski, Patrice Heber, and Elyse Nakajima—for your help and support through Enneagram Institute certification and teaching.

We're thankful as well to Mario Sikora and Maria Jose Munita for your Awareness to Action teachings on applying the Enneagram to business and coaching in an accessible way.

Thank you to Deb Ooten, Beth O'Hara, Tom Condon, David Daniels, and Jessica Dibb for your insightful workshops and wise counsel and support.

Big thanks to Nana K. Twumasi and the Callisto Media team for giving us a wonderful opportunity to write about the Enneagram and offer a fresh take on its valuable teachings.

Gratitude to Shut Up and Write San Francisco for being a welcoming environment to get much of this book written.

Our parents and brothers have been supportive of our interest in the Enneagram and put up with a lot of "number conversations" over the years. A huge thank you to them all!

Melanie would like to thank Katherine Fauvre and David Fauvre for their early mentorship, the Renaissance College faculty and staff for nurturing the exploration of leadership in different contexts, and Thomas Mengel for supervising my first Enneagram research and workshops. Thank you to Ricky Germain for introducing me to the Enneagram and for many interesting discussions, and to Aine ni Cheallaigh for writing and type talk.

Kacie would like to thank Earl Wagner and Anne Geary for collaboration, discussion, and friendship. Our discussions over the years have been enriching and fulfilling. Thank you to Bonnie Hamilton, Richelle and Fo McKinley, and Scott Valeri for friendship and support at Enneagram events and beyond.

Last but not least, we would like to thank each other for the years of collaboration, innovation, love, and support. May there be many more!

ABOUT THE AUTHORS

Melanie Bell, MA, is an Enneagram Institute Authorized Teacher, writer, and international speaker. As Director of Teaching for Berghoef & Bell Innovations, she has created curricula and led workshops across disciplines and continents. A coach and university writing instructor, she holds degrees in Interdisciplinary Leadership from the University of New Brunswick and in Creative Writing from Concordia University. Her creative writing and columns have appeared in a number of publications including *xoJane*, *Grain*, *The Fiddlehead*, and *Autostraddle*.

Kacie Berghoef, MSW, is an Enneagram Institute Authorized Teacher, freelance writer, and international speaker. As Director of Management for Berghoef & Bell Innovations, she has planned and co-facilitated workshops for business, spiritual, and community audiences. Kacie holds an MSW from UC Berkeley and a BA in Philosophy from Scripps College. She works as a professional blogger and copywriter for businesses and Enneagram clients. Her writing has appeared in *Personality Revealed*, *The Billfold*, *Mapquest*, *Skirt Collective*, and *Nine Points Magazine*. She enjoys developing and researching new Enneagram applications.